Sticky Faith Curriculum

FULLER YOUTH INSTITUTE
Can I Ask That?
8 Hard Questions about God and Faith
LEADER GUIDE
A Sticky Faith Curriculum

Published in the United States of America by
Fuller Youth Institute, 135 N. Oakland Ave., Pasadena, CA, 91182
fulleryouthinstitute.org

ISBN 978-0-9914880-0-1

Cover and Interior Design: Matthew Schuler, Fuller Youth Institute
Cover Photo: Katie Swayze

Copy Editor: Joy Thompson
Printed in the United States of America

CAN

8 HARD QUESTIONS ABOUT GOD & FAITH

I ASK

A STICKY FAITH CURRICULUM

THAT?

JIM CANDY, BRAD M. GRIFFIN, KARA POWELL

Top tips for reading your Bible   Letter for parents & footnotes

Stephen was in his first week at college.

He was interested in a class he'd signed up for called "The Bible as Literature." The professor seemed really fun and obviously brilliant. Stephen figured she probably knew pretty much everything about the Bible.

"Welcome to class," Dr. Swanson smiled at the start of the opening session. "We're going to begin with Jonah."

The students stopped staring at their phones and looked up. It only took Stephen about ten seconds to notice the girl two chairs over from him. He *knew* there would be hot girls in college.

"Many of you have heard the Bible story of Jonah, a man who was swallowed by a big fish," Dr. Swanson continued. "But does anyone here actually *believe* that happened?"

Stephen looked around the class to see if anyone else would raise their hand. No one did and, most importantly, the hot girl kept her hand down ... so he didn't raise his hand either.

"Exactly," the professor continued. "There's no way Jonah could have been swallowed by a fish. It's just a literary device."

A literary device?

The professor explained how ancient writers used stories like this to illustrate a point. In fact, the prof continued, the story of Jonah was similar to *other stories* written by other ancient writers. Not only was it not a real story, but it was just a borrowed story from ancient fiction.

Inside, Stephen panicked.

Why didn't my youth leaders at church talk to me about this in high school? Were they hiding something? he wondered. *Is this professor telling the truth?*

As the prof continued, Stephen started wondering if the entire Bible fit the category she assigned to Jonah: *fiction*. He had always loved his church and Jesus as best he could, but his whole world was suddenly filled with doubt about his faith.

Surprised at himself, Stephen started to ask himself a deeper question.

Is faith in God something you do when you're a kid, just until you know better?

Why this
study?

The above story is an example of the reality that awaits high schoolers as they take their faith into the adult world. In fact, many young people deal with intense challenges to their faith earlier in high school or middle school. Having listened to the questions of teenagers, we developed these eight sessions to explore openly some of the issues that teenagers are waiting for adults to take seriously.

Research indicates that about five of every ten high schoolers will walk away from the church and their faith after graduation. Because of that tragedy, the team at the Fuller Youth Institute set out to discover how to help young people develop a faith that lasts, or what we call **Sticky Faith**.

As we learned in our research, there are a variety of reasons a young person might leave faith behind as they cross that bridge:

Some leave because other things become more important to them.

Visit stickyfaith.org for more details and all kinds of resources for youth leaders and parents.

Some leave over a bad experience in a youth group.

Some leave as they seek independence from the opinions of their parents.

Some leave because they never really felt like part of the church to begin with.

And some leave because the church fails to prepare them adequately for life beyond high school.

These sessions aim to help parents, youth workers, and any adult who cares about teenagers to engage them on a level that takes their developing faith seriously.

One recent survey [1] asked leaders of campus-based atheist clubs why they don't believe in God. Their responses were revealing:

Many had actually been involved in a youth ministry during their high school years.

They named the church's failure to engage difficult questions as a key reason they left.

Specifically, these young people cited the church's failure to wrestle with issues like the reliability of the biblical text, sexuality, evolution versus creation, and the exclusivity of Jesus. But notice these students did *not* say they left the faith because of the *stance their church took* on the issues above. *They left because the church failed to address them at all.* When tough questions were addressed, the answers were found to be vague and superficial.

The study on which you are embarking will be challenging. It was challenging to write, and challenging for the groups who field-tested these sessions in their own ministries. These eight topics not only will push your students, but probably will push you too. There are few easy answers. You likely will notice points where you're forced to live with the tension of saying, "I don't know." When that happens, remember: **saying "I don't know" is better than avoidance.**

Teenagers will ask these questions with or without you.

Let it be *with* you. In taking this study seriously, your credibility will increase in the eyes of your students. And, more importantly, the credibility of the gospel of Jesus Christ will increase as well. By being willing to entertain hard questions, you present both yourself and Jesus as safe and trustworthy. Our prayer is that the Holy Spirit will move deeply among your group as you wrestle with some of the faith's deepest and most challenging questions in our day and across time.

▬ ▬ ▬

The eight sessions tackle the following tough questions:

- ⊗ *Can I trust the Bible?*
- ⊗ *Does the Bible contradict itself?*
- ⊗ *Can I be a Christian and believe in evolution?*
- ⊗ *Does God discriminate against women?*
- ⊗ *Is Jesus really the only way to God?*
- ⊗ *What does the Bible say about being gay?*
- ⊗ *Does God endorse violence?*
- ⊗ *How can I follow a God who would let Christians do such bad things?*

What you should know
before you start

Here are five important keys to help teenagers engage this study right out of the gate.

KEY #1:
This is about faith that sticks.

Sticky Faith is an initiative from the Fuller Youth Institute designed to understand and help faith "stick" in teenagers (see stickyfaith.org for more info and resources). In other words, we want to see young people grow in faith in Christ as they grow into adults. We have observed through research that wrestling with doubt—even doubt in God— can be a very healthy process. We hope this curriculum helps you have real conversations with God and each other about difficult topics.

KEY #2: Don't hold back.

Encourage teenagers that *any* questions or doubts are welcome. In fact, they are required. Let students be honest. See what God might do in them—and you—through this process. God is not biting fingernails, nervous about the tough questions this study raises. God is also not going to be angry or annoyed by doubt. We have a big God.

KEY #3:
Help them learn the "context."

To understand what the Bible means, we need to understand

what it meant for the people who wrote and read it "way back then." Studying the "context" means discovering who wrote the Bible, to whom they wrote, and why.

For example, imagine a high school student is in class and her phone buzzes. Someone texted her from a number she doesn't recognize:

I've been secretly wanting to ask you this for a while now ... Prom?

Because she doesn't recognize who sent it, she doesn't know whether to be excited or angry. The author and their intentions are unknown. Is it a friend playing a joke on her from someone else's phone? Is it the guy she dreams about? Was it sent to her accidentally?

Without the *context* of this mystery text message, she doesn't know what it means. The Bible is the same way. We need to know who wrote the passage (as much as is possible), why they wrote it, and for what individual or community it was written. Context is crucial for

understanding a passage. For that reason, every session will have a section on "Context."

KEY #4: Don't study alone.

These sessions are meant to be used in a group, not alone. As a leader, *read through the session before you meet.* **Let's repeat that: Please read the Leader Guide before each session.** This will deepen your conversation and help you anticipate questions when you meet with the group. There are more tips below on how to lead the sessions logistically.

KEY #5: Ask God for help.

Leading these sessions will bring up challenging questions and potentially big breakthroughs for you and the teenagers you are leading. Jesus promises the Holy Spirit lives in us to help us make sense of the scriptures. Take God up on this promise, and ask the Holy Spirit to guide you as you lead.

Checklist for leading

this study

☐ Each student has a copy of the *Student Guide.*

☐ Each student has the opportunity to read through the session *before* the group meeting (this is ideal, but optional). There are pros and cons to sending books home with students. The biggest pro is that they'll be more likely to read the content before and/or after your meetings, and they'll have notes from your discussion to refer back to. But the obvious con is that they'll forget them and show up without a guide. You might want to decide based on what you already know about your students, or experiment and see how it goes.

☐ Leaders have read the *Leader Guide* and are familiar with the topic and potential direction the conversation may go. Look for the "LEADER NOTES" In sprinkled throughout the Leader Guide for specific ideas and tips. If you're the youth pastor or organizational leader, you will probably want to gather all of your small group leaders together to talk through the study and highlight issues where your church would want to communicate clearly about particular ideas or positions.

☐ You have emailed parents with a letter similar to the one found at the end of this Leader Guide. *Very important*: The different opinions surrounding the topics of these sessions can lead to controversy. It is wise to address your intentions for this study directly with parents and other key leaders in your church/organization ahead of time. Also, please note that this study is intended for high school students. Middle school students may or may not be ready for these topics.

Study 4
format

Each session is formatted to help students dive into the topic through the following progression:

△   ***Sticky Story:*** A relevant, realistic story designed to get teenagers talking, much like the one at the beginning of this introduction.

q   ***Sticky Questions:*** Initial questions to unearth students' current opinions on the topic.

n   ***Sticky Notes:*** A dialogue with background context and other factors that influence how people understand the issue. In this section we also share various and often opposing viewpoints within the Christian community or broader culture.

s   ***Sticking with the Scripture:*** Relevant scripture and questions about each topic.

t   ***Sticky Talk:*** Fictional conversations that capture the essence of the issue and opinions surrounding it.

All scripture referenced in the study is from the New International Version (NIV) unless otherwise noted, but feel free to use your preferred Bible translation in your small group discussions.

How to lead these

$$\boxed{5}$$

A few tips for leading the sessions from week to week:

* This conversation guide works *way* better if your group knows each other before the study. If your group is new or has a few new members who don't know the others well, spend a little time at the beginning on some kind of "get to know you" exercise. Food also helps!

* These sessions are written to help you guide the discussion in such a way that honors the theological leaning of your particular tradition. Obviously, express your opinion on each matter, but we encourage you *not* to short-circuit the dialogue for students who might disagree with your position.

* Each session is designed to take about one hour.

* Read through the opening story out loud as a group to highlight the importance of the topic and spur conversation. Invite different students to read different sections and pose the questions throughout.

* Be okay with saying the words, "I don't know." Be okay with occasional moments of awkward silence as well. Both are important when weighty matters are on the table.

* Resist the temptation to answer every question your teenagers pose. Sometimes it is best to ask them to think more about it or to research their questions on their own. Then offer to buy them lunch

and talk about it later!

* You might want to close each session by handing out notecards and inviting students to write down one question they still have about the topic at hand or any previous topic you've discussed. Sometimes students will share in writing what they don't dare to say out loud.

* Invite a co-leader to join you. Given the diversity of life experience, tradition, and opinion that probably exists within your church, two leaders can enrich your group's dialogue.

* Consider letting the students know that their friends who don't believe in God are welcome to join the group. In our testing of this study, some students found this to be a great opportunity to bring pre-Christian friends for honest and open dialogue about faith.

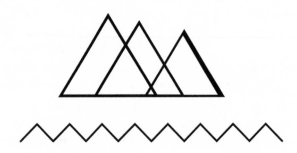

One final note about interpretation: While we've attempted to present well-balanced approaches to these tricky topics, it's inevitable that some of our own biases and beliefs will come through in these lessons. Our own traditions include Presbyterian, Methodist, Nazarene, Assemblies of God, and Congregational backgrounds. We also field tested these sessions and invited critical readers and input from other backgrounds, like Baptists, Evangelical Free, and non-denominational churches.

Though our views might seep through—as will yours when you lead your group through the study—our hope is that a variety of viewpoints can be discussed and scripture can be studied in such a way that students arrive at their own views. And while you may go into this hoping students will come out on the other side with "right" beliefs, it may be that the most important part of this whole journey is the process itself.

That's worth saying again.

It may be that the most important part of this whole journey is the process itself.

Session

1 Can I trust the Bible?

Big Idea

Students will wrestle with whether—and how much—the content of the New Testament was changed along the way before it became the Bible we have today.

 (*leader notes*)

This may be your students' first time hearing about this particular issue (and perhaps this is your first time tackling it with a group!). Give them background about why the Church believes the Bible is a reliable document, but also ask them to consider how reading the Bible might change their faith and life. Let them ask questions and raise doubts, and don't be afraid of not being an authority on the subject of biblical authorship. When your students ask tough questions you can't answer, you can always do some research (ideally with them) and get back to the group at your next meeting.

Note that while we use the term "Bible" in the title for the sake of simplicity, we are predominantly focused on the reliability of the *New Testament* in this session as an introduction to how the Bible came to us from the early church.

You'll Need

In (*leader notes*)

⊗ Your copy of this **Leader Guide** and a **Student Guide** for each participant.

⊗ A pencil or pen for each participant.

⊗ This session will require you to do some study up front. *Be sure* to look over this leader guide thoroughly and familiarize yourself with these concepts. If you have never studied the history of the formation of the books of the Bible before, you might want to do some additional reading to learn a bit more than this study provides.

⊗ A flipchart or a big piece of paper and a marker.

Start by having a student read the following story out loud.

Brett was the guy you never thought would walk away from God.

He was "Mr. Youth Group" – never missed a meeting, camp, or mission trip. EVERYTHING the church did, Brett was there. He even helped in the children's ministry and served as a camp leader.

He knew the Bible really well too. His parents had taught Brett a lot about the Bible, and he was one of those kids who seemed to get it. Most people thought Brett would become a pastor when he graduated from college.

But that all changed during Brett's senior year of high school.

Brett decided to write his final senior project on how the New Testament was written. He started searching the Internet for sources, and found a scholar who is well-known for his biblical knowledge. This scholar had written many books. Brett was thrilled to learn from someone this well respected on something he cared about so much.

As he read through the scholar's blog, he found a post that seemed like just what he was looking for. But as he read, Brett was surprised and somewhat concerned by the perspective shared by the author.

> *Has anyone played the game telephone? Telephone is the game when people pass a phrase around a circle by whispering into the next person's ear. Usually the message ends up very different by the time the phrase reaches the last person. Now, take a moment and imagine a giant game of telephone that lasts for centuries. That is the Bible.*

Brett was intrigued. He had never thought about how the Bible was actually put together. He always just assumed the books of the Bible were all stored together in a museum somewhere.

"Now," the blog post continued, "I find it curious that some people actually bet their whole lives on a game of telephone." The next section was titled "The Truth about the New Testament" and listed all the reasons this writer believed the New Testament can't be trusted. [2]

Brett started wondering... *Am I betting my life on a telephone game?*

What he read on the blog ...

- ⊗ *We have no original copies of the New Testament books—only copies of copies.*

- ⊗ *The first copy we have of any part of the New Testament is from around the year 200 A.D.*

- ⊗ *People made mistakes when copying the Bible.*

- ⊗ *There are 300,000 changes in the Bible among all the different copies.*

 In *(leader notes)*

Ask your group for any big observations from the story and move quickly to the next section.

 (*questions*)

 (*leader notes*)

Listen intently during these first questions. How, if at all, have the members of your group been impacted at school and elsewhere by this topic? Whatever your personal opinion, resist the temptation to share your thoughts in the beginning of each session. Make sure your group feels the freedom to express their own thoughts before you share yours.

> What do you know already about how the New Testament was written? What have you heard?

> Does it matter if the Bible has been significantly changed since its original letters and books were written? Why or why not?

 (*leader notes*)

You will likely find that most of your students have not dealt with this topic much before. Yet it is also highly likely that teenagers will be faced with this question as they progress in high school and beyond. Talking about this now helps your students avoid being surprised when it comes up along the way.

In *(leader notes)*

You may want to guide the conversation to focus on the overall narrative that plays out in scripture. The New Testament contains the history of God actually coming to earth as a person in Jesus Christ. The New Testament is not just a collection of sayings from a good teacher. If the Bible has been significantly changed, it might be difficult to have confidence in the main message of Christianity: *God entered the world in the person of Jesus to make all things right with God.*

> Read the blog notes again from the opening story. What if those notes were all true? What does this make you think? How does it make you feel?

In *(leader notes)*

These points may sound surprising at first, but they do not necessarily discredit biblical integrity, especially when compared to other ancient literature. Looking at the list on the previous page, point by point:

* We have no original copies of the New Testament letters and gospels. The original books written by Paul, the gospel writers and other authors have not been found. But we also don't have the originals of any other ancient work from that period.

* The gospels and letters of the New Testament were written by different people in different places at different times. The stories of Jesus captured in the gospels were first passed down orally prior to being written down. But it's important to know that in the ancient world, this was how all stories were carefully preserved. In the modern

world, "telephone" games don't work because we aren't an oral culture, but that's not true of the ancient world.

* The first copy of a fragment, or part, of the New Testament in existence is from around the year 200 A.D. Not all scholars agree on the timeline, but it is generally believed the original manuscripts were all completed by the year 90 A.D.

* People made mistakes when copying the Bible. Almost no scholars would argue that scribes did not make some "variances" when they copied the New Testament. The question is: How important were they? Continue this session for more help with this question.

* There are around 300,000 changes that have been noted among all the existing copies of scriptural texts. Scholars who cite this number add up all the variances initially made by scribes but then also include all subsequent copies, making the number seem more inflated.

In summary, archaeological discoveries have generally affirmed the reliability of the transmission of scripture over time. In the 1900s, the Dead Sea Scrolls were found, which confirmed that the Old Testament texts had not been significantly modified in the thousand years between when the Dead Sea Scrolls were written and when the next-oldest existing texts (the Masoretic Texts) were written (see deadseascrolls. org or deadseascrolls.org.il for more background.)

Even a quick web search comparing New Testament reliability to that of other ancient literature reveals that we have far more existing copies of the New Testament than other ancient literature. Additionally, the time span between the New Testament's writing and our first surviving copies is far shorter than the time span between the writing and first existing copies of many other ancient works. [3]

> If you were in a conversation with this blogging professor, what would you say or ask? Why?

In *(leader notes)*

This section requires your advance study. Listen to students' answers and then hand out a copy of the picture below. It is an excerpt of one of the oldest papyri in existence that contains almost the entire gospel of John. It is dated near 200 A.D.

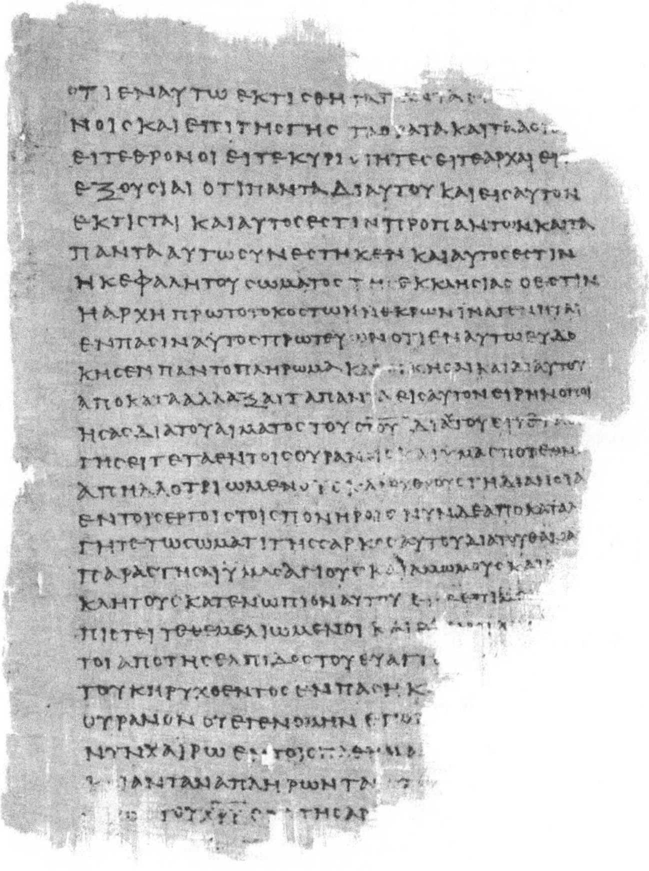

> What do you notice about what's written on this paper?

 (leader notes)

— — — — — — — — — — — — —

Make sure they get the following points:

* It's Greek, not English! (The New Testament was written in Greek; the Old Testament in Hebrew and Aramaic.)

* There are no chapter titles, verses, or explanatory footnotes. Those were added later.

* There are no punctuation marks.

* It was handwritten, not typed (let alone spell-checked on a computer!).

> How would you guess something like this papyrus written 1,800 years ago became the Bible you have in your hand today?

 (leader notes)

— — — — — — — — — — — — —

Let them respond...

Now it's time for you to do a little teaching. If you're not an expert, DON'T worry. This guide will walk you through enough background for the sake of this session. Draw the following diagram on a piece of paper or flipchart:

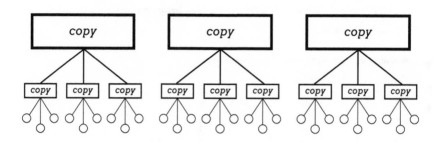

Original Greek Manuscript of each New Testament Book

Help students understand that you are showing how the Bible was transmitted over time. There were no printing presses until Gutenberg's invention introduced mass printing in the 15th century! Until then, all copies of books were written by hand, usually by people trained as "scribes." Now ask:

1. What happens if one scribe is out too late the night before and makes a spelling error? Circle one of the copies in the chart when you do this. Then ask, **What happens to the following copies after that one?**

Point out that once a scribe makes a mistake or "variance," all the subsequent copies will have the same variance. When biblical scholars count variances, they count the original variance and all the variances copied from that original.

2. How do we know what were the original words of the New Testament if there are changes?

Help students see that scholars can compare manuscripts to determine the original words of the Bible. In fact, scholars have spent thousands of hours doing this for English translations of the Greek and Hebrew portions of the Bible.

(leader notes)

— — — — — — — — — — — —

Below are some questions we encountered while testing this study with high schoolers. We imagine you might also encounter them:

> *I've heard there are other "Gnostic Gospels" (like the Gospel of Thomas). Why weren't they included in the Bible we use today?*

> *What is the "canon"?*

The early church used proximity to Jesus' life and eyewitnesses to help determine which books were included in the scriptures and which were not. The Gnostic (the root word means "knowledge" in Greek) Gospels were written later by a group that claimed "secret knowledge" about Jesus. The early church rejected the idea that Jesus' teachings were only for a privileged few who understood this secret knowledge. Many scholars believe the books of the New Testament were all originally written by about 90 AD, within approximately 60 years of Jesus' life, death, and resurrection.

The "canon" means the books of the Bible believed to be genuine. The biblical canon is comprised of the books the early church believed to be the accurate and true New and Old Testaments. Many believe the New Testament canon was set by the middle of the 3rd century, according to evidence we have in letters from early church fathers. Note, however, that the Roman Catholic canon includes a few books that Protestant churches eventually excluded, so there's still some difference in opinion today about canonicity. [4]

How do we know the Bible wasn't changed before our earliest existing manuscripts?

We don't. But according to the standards of other ancient literature, we have our first copies of New Testament texts very close to the time they were originally written. New Testament scholar John Montgomery states, "To be skeptical of ... the New Testament books is to let all of classical antiquity slip into obscurity, for no documents of the ancient period are as well attested bibliographically as the New Testament." [5]

When you're done with this section, you may want to just ask students to read these Sticky Notes on their own or point out to them the quotes from Bart Ehrman or F. F. Bruce. Note: Ehrman is one of the biggest proponents of the "telephone" theory and argues that the Bible is unreliable. It is useful to introduce your students to these arguments now, with you, rather than leaving them to discover these theories on their own later. You may want to peruse Ehrman's book, *Misquoting Jesus,* to familiarize yourself with his ideas. Additionally, there are numerous short videos of Ehrman on the Internet explaining his perspective.

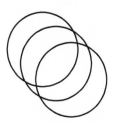

n *(notes)*

Why does this matter?

Some people don't care if the Bible was changed through the years. They see it as a book with helpful thoughts from good teachers.

But the Bible is much more. The Bible contains the history of God and God's people over time, including the account of God actually coming to earth as a person: Jesus Christ.

If the Bible has been *significantly* changed, it might be difficult to have confidence in the main messages of scripture about who God is and who we are.

How did we get the Bible we have today?

Although we believe the Bible is inspired by God, it didn't magically appear. God used normal people to write the Bible. Most scholars believe all the New Testament writings were completed within a handful of decades after Jesus' death and resurrection. The New Testament writers had access either to Jesus or to eyewitnesses of Jesus. People called "scribes" copied down the words of the Bible over many centuries.

Did the scribes ever mess up? What goofs did they make?

CONTEXT!

Is it unusual that the Bible was copied by hand over the years? Answer: No.

Every ancient book was copied. Why? No photocopy machines or printing presses! The Bible has been copied by hand and eventually copied in print *more than any other book in history.*

Did every person who copied the Bible over the centuries do it with 100% accuracy? Few argue that every scribe did it perfectly and never made a mistake. The more important question is: What kind of changes (called "*variances*") are there?

What Kinds of Changes Did Scribes Make?

There *are* examples of scribes making changes as they copied the texts.

Bart Ehrman, a widely recognized New Testament scholar (who does not claim to be a Christian), notes that the Bible has many "copy errors." However, Ehrman admits most differences don't significantly change the meaning of those texts:

"Most of these differences we have in our manuscripts are completely insignificant, unimportant and don't matter for a thing." [6] *- Bart Ehrman*

However, Ehrman believes some changes **do** affect how we read the Bible, like changes in the ways passages might be interpreted by shifting a word or two.

(leader notes)

Ehrman holds that some scribes changed texts in an attempt to emphasize the divinity of Jesus. One example includes passages in Luke 2 that do not refer to Jesus' father. Ehrman contends that early scribes, defending the divinity of Jesus, changed the word "father" and instead used the name Joseph as a way to eliminate arguments that Jesus was not born to a virgin. College students will likely be exposed to arguments like this so it is helpful to familiarize yourself and prepare them.

> So are the scriptures we now have faithful to the "original" Bible texts or not?

It's a complicated question, but most Christian scholars agree the answer is YES. One problem with the "telephone" argument is that *we still have many of the early copies* that affirm later copies. Even if a scribe ***did*** make a mistake, we often have an earlier copy to compare. Another problem is that the biblical writings came out of primarily oral cultures, meaning people verbally shared stories in a whole different (and more consistent) way than we do today.

QUOTE

"The evidence for our New Testament writings is ever so much greater than the evidence of any writings of the classical authors, the authenticity of which no one dreams of questioning." [7]
— F.F. Bruce, New Testament Scholar (Bruce and other scholars are comparing the New Testament to classical works by authors such as Plato, Homer and Aristotle).

> Why do we have so many translations now?

Different people have taken early manuscripts and attempted to translate the Greek words (or Hebrew in the Old Testament) into Latin, then later English and other languages. Also, over time the church came to agreement about which books were part of the authoritative Bible and which were not considered part of scripture. The Bible we have today is a product of those individuals, councils, Bible translators, and scholars through the years. But within the English language, for example, there are multiple translations of the Bible because different groups of scholars make different translation choices. That's because ancient languages often don't have exact English equivalents.

In (*leader notes*)

Lead your students out of this section by saying something like, **Let's look at one more scripture passage that shows in a different way why all of this matters.**

S *(scripture)*

Most Christian traditions believe the Bible is God's inspired word to humanity. The Holy Spirit inspired human authors to capture God's Word and communicate it to God's people in specific places and times, as well as over time to us. Because we believe it's God's word, scripture has "authority" in our lives. The Holy Spirit uses scripture to shape us into people who live in relationship with—and try to live like—Jesus Christ.

The Bible is inspired by God for a *purpose*. Yes, it is designed to show us what happened and when. But it is also designed to *change us.* The apostle Paul wrote the following words prior to the creation of the entire New Testament we have today, but he still speaks to this reality when he writes:

There's nothing like the written Word of God for showing you the way to salvation through faith in Christ Jesus. Every part of Scripture is God-breathed and useful one way or another—showing us truth, exposing our rebellion, correcting our mistakes, training us to live God's way. Through the Word we are put together and shaped up for the tasks God has for us.

– 2 Timothy 3:15-17 (The Message)

What do you think about the ways this passage claims the Bible is "useful"?

In what ways have specific Bible passages helped you to grow as a Christ-follower?

How has the Bible been hard for you to understand?

 In *(leader notes)*

It will be fascinating to see how many of your students actually read the Bible, and if they can name experiences with the Bible that have helped them grow.

Some students, if they're really honest, will say that they have not had very good experiences with reading the Bible. Thank them for being honest about that, and let them know it's not uncommon to find the Bible confusing and complicated. At the same time, the Bible is written to reveal more about God and God's story to us, so the more we explore it, the more we will understand over time.

(*talk*)

  (*leader notes*)

— — — — — — — — — — — —

In each session we want to make sure students understand why this particular issue might matter for them and their own faith development. We've created the following dialogue to help highlight different perspectives. Invite your students to create their own dialogue with these characters and with each other.

Pretend you are with some friends who start talking about God. Read their viewpoints and follow the instructions below.

WILL

I think Jesus is real and I don't understand why it matters if the Bible was changed or not. Almost everyone agrees that he was a real person and that he did amazing things. Why are we so worried over a few words in the Bible here and there? In fact, I'm not convinced that it really matters that Jesus was a real person. Can't we just live the way he taught us to live and not argue over a few changes in the Bible?

KIRSTEN

It's absolutely critical that the words in the Bible are the exact words of Jesus. If there is even one word that is not a direct quote, how can we trust that anything is accurate in the Bible? There are people out there who just don't like Christianity and are trying to make the Bible look bad.

MILES

All this study of the Bible is fine, but the big question is, "Would God allow us to have an unreliable record of his story?" God knew we would need a way to understand what it means to follow Jesus. I trust God enough to believe that we have the Bible we were supposed to get.

JESSICA

All these professors and scholars know way more than I do about the Bible. I have no idea how I'll ever tell what is right or wrong if the Bible was changed. So since I can't tell what is true or not, I am not sure if the Bible is true. How can anyone be totally sure? There are smart people who disagree on this stuff. Maybe they are all right and nobody is really wrong.

Instructions

⊗ Take a pencil or pen and *underline* any thoughts the characters shared that you agree with. Why do you agree?

⊗ Take a pencil or pen and *circle* the thoughts you disagree with. Why do you disagree?

⊗ Share with the group why you circled and underlined what you did. Be open to learning something here from your leaders and other group members!

> Do you have any other questions right now about this topic? What are they?

> My opinion on this topic (at least for now) is ...

 In (*leader notes*)

Ask your group for brief thoughts about the next session's topic so you can be thinking about any particular needs your group may have in your approach.

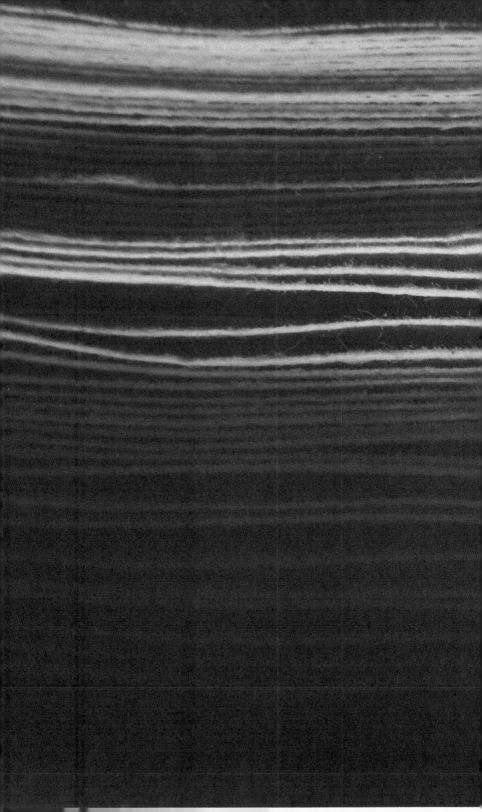

Session

2

Does the Bible contradict itself?

Big Idea

Students will be exposed to the argument that the Bible is internally inconsistent because some of the stories don't line up well, and wrestle with how to interpret these differences as we read the Bible.

— — —

You'll Need

In *(leader notes)*

⊗ Your copy of this Leader Guide and a Student Guide for each participant.

⊗ A pencil or pen for each participant.

Ruth was friends with everyone.

People thought she was fun. Guys thought Ruth was cute. Her coaches thought she would get a scholarship in tennis. She was the "All American" kid. She was kind to other people too. Her teachers loved her. She got along with everyone.

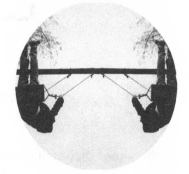

Everyone but Annaliese.

Annaliese was quieter and not as well known at her high school, but she would ask Ruth questions that bugged her. Ruth didn't believe in God, and Annaliese was a Christian. Annaliese would often ask questions like, "If there is no God, what is life really about, Ruth?" Asking this once or twice was no big deal, but Annaliese would ask this question, or a version of it, often. Ruth thought it was annoying.

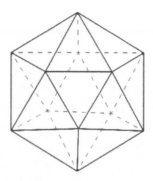

But sometimes it also made Ruth wonder. *Why* don't *I believe in God?*

Ruth's parents had always told her that the Bible was a book of nice stories, but once you studied it, you found out there were lots of contradictions. She decided to ask Annaliese about it.

"I have trouble believing God exists because I've heard the Bible gets its stories mixed up," Ruth said. "How can Christians say this book is from God when there are different accounts of the same story? I don't trust it."

"Where did you hear there are conflicting stories in the Bible?" Annaliese replied. "That's not true. Show me where."

So for a class project, Ruth decided to find contradicting passages in the Bible. She started with the resurrection of Jesus. *"If I can show Annaliese there are different accounts of the resurrection of Jesus, then I will finally win this ridiculous argument,"* she thought.

Ruth read Matthew, Mark, Luke and John's stories about Jesus' resurrection and found several discrepancies in the stories. She made the following chart for her class assignment to show the different ways each author wrote about the resurrection of Jesus.

Ruth shared her chart with Annaliese before she turned it in for her class. The chart surprised Annaliese. She went home and compared her Bible to Ruth's chart. It seemed to Annaliese there were differences after all.

Annaliese wondered, *Does this mean Ruth is right? Does the Bible have stories that don't agree with each other?*

What was Annaliese supposed to do with this new information?

	Matthew	Mark	Luke	John
Women who came to the tomb...	Mary Magdalene and the other Mary	Mary Magdalene and the other Mary	Mary Magdalene, the other Mary, & Joanna	Only Mary Magdalene
The tomb's entrance stone...	Angel appeared and rolled it away	Stone already had been moved	Stone already had been moved	Stone already had been moved
Angelic appearance...	Dressed in white – like lightning	Young man dressed in white	Two men like "lightning"	Two angels in white
The women felt...	Afraid but with great joy	Astonished and afraid; run away	Frightened	Mary doesn't seem afraid

(questions)

Why does this topic matter?

 (leader notes)

— — — — — — — — — — — —

If the Biblical writers had conflicting stories, how can we trust its record? If we are basing our lives on what scripture says about Jesus' life, death, and resurrection, we need to know we have reliable witnesses to that story.

If you had a friend like Ruth who handed you this chart, what would you say or ask?

 (leader notes)

— — — — — — — — — — — —

Encourage students to deal with two issues:

1. How do we account for these apparent inconsistencies in the gospels that Ruth discovered? (The Sticky Notes section will help with this question).

2. How is Annaliese handling herself in this process? Is she moving Ruth toward or away from God? This will be an interesting discussion because, on the one hand, it doesn't appear God would call us to "annoy" people about what we believe. On the other hand, Annaliese is playing a "prophetic" role in Ruth's life.

3. Are debates about "proof" helpful in talking with others about our faith? What role do you think debate should play in your conversations with others about faith?

How important is it to you that the Bible's authors agree 100 percent on every detail? Explain your answer.

 (leader notes)

— — — — — — — — — — — — — —

Let them answer! Hold your opinion for now. But feel free to contradict what students say at times in order to get your group thinking more deeply.

Who is a Christian you respect? What do they think about this topic? (Ask them this week before or after the group meets!)

 (leader notes)

— — — — — — — — — — — — — —

Transition to the next section, letting participants take turns reading aloud.

(notes)

Different perspectives

In court, witnesses give testimony. Often the accounts don't match. Does this mean nothing happened? Or could it mean they saw or heard the situation differently?

Jesus' resurrection story is an example of different writers giving their own views. Some people believe this actually *increases* the trustworthiness of the Bible because it shows the writers did not conspire to invent a perfect story. Further, the gospel writers were writing to different communities with different questions and concerns. They wanted to communicate not only *what* happened, but also *why* it was so important. Sort of like the way you tell a story differently when you're sharing it with your best friend or writing it for journalism class.

Inerrancy vs. Infallibility

Here are two fancy words describing how different people view the Bible's accuracy:

Inerrancy: This position holds that the Bible is without any factual error. The Bible is inspired by God and, therefore, all facts are completely accurate, even those that seem to contradict.

Infallibility: This position teaches that the Bible is inspired by God but may contain some factual or technical errors. However, those errors do not change the message of the Bible nor its purpose as God's authoritative Word to human beings.

Both perspectives believe in the authority of God's Word.

These are not the only two ways to view the reliability of scripture, but two common ways that churches and individual Christians tend to interpret what they read.

> How else might someone explain differences between the stories of the Bible?

> What do you think is the main point of the resurrection story?

> Do you think the different accounts shown in Ruth's chart weaken or strengthen that point, or make any difference given that main point?

> Are there many other places where the writers' stories don't seem to fit together?

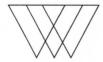

Here are a few other passages to check out:

> * Read Matthew 27:3-8 and Acts 1:18-19 (two accounts of Judas' death)
>
> * Read 1 Samuel 31:4-6 and 2 Samuel 1:6-10 (two accounts of Saul's death)
>
> *A number of stories or parables of Jesus differ slightly or significantly among the four gospels. Try to find the same story in more than one of the gospels and look for any differences between them. For example, read the accounts of Jesus feeding 5,000 people in Matthew 14:13-21, Mark 6:30-44, Luke 9:10-17, and John 6:1-13.

CONTEXT!

When you read about a baseball game, the journalist often includes attendance figures. If it's the San Francisco Giants, the attendance is often around 42,031. These are *exact* numbers based on ticket sales.

Were Biblical writers as precise as modern writers? Or was the culture's take on recording numbers different? When the Bible says Jesus fed 5,000, did someone count? Or did they only count men, but not women and children? Or was the author just making the point that it was a *really big* crowd? The way you answer these questions is important; some believe the writers may not have been as concerned with exact detail as we are. Others disagree and believe God's inspiration means every detail is correct. Still others say the different writers were concerned about recording different things. (Ever read the book of Numbers? Open it now just for fun.)

As scribes were copying and recopying versions of the gospels, why wouldn't they have "cleaned up" the differences between the accounts of the gospel writers?

 (*leader notes*)

If students are stumped here, this is a good time to reinforce that different writers may have been writing for different reasons as they communicated with different audiences. The scribes were more aware of those nuances than the average reader might be two thousand years later. The next section will explore this a bit more.

(scripture)

The beauty of the Bible is that God used ordinary people to write different parts of God's story—a story that would be shared for centuries. All of these writers were different, and had various reasons for writing down what they had seen or heard. Read Luke's take on why he wrote his version of the gospel to Theophilus and the community in which Theophilus lived:

> *Many have undertaken to draw up an account of the things that have been fulfilled among us, just as they were handed down to us by those who from the first were eyewitnesses and servants of the word. With this in mind, since I myself have carefully investigated everything from the beginning, I too decided to write an orderly account for you, most excellent Theophilus, so that you may know the certainty of the things you have been taught.*
>
> — Luke 1:1-4

Luke wrote this on papyrus paper. He didn't have a "cover page" or an editor, and there was no graphic designer to make it look cool. Often writers in ancient times would treat the opening sentence of a letter like we use the cover of a book today. They put really important information that they wanted to make sure people read and understood right at the front. So these first few sentences in Luke are important.

What is the main point of Luke's opening statement above?

What kind of confidence does that give you in the author's story?

 In *(leader notes)*

Your group will probably not linger for long on these two questions. Also, it is likely that someone will ask, "It seems like we're using the Bible to prove the Bible is accurate. Isn't that wrong?"

Encourage them for asking that question. It is a good point. However, also help them see that Luke took his job seriously as a writer and consulted eyewitnesses and others to get his story straight. But at some point we also have to decide if we trust Luke as a witness who captured all of this for us in writing, and if we trust that God inspired these words.

What does it mean for *you* to be credible in how you share Jesus?

Luke is sharing the story about Jesus Christ. He wants his readers to know why he is a credible source. Whether or not we realize it, we are also like Luke. We also share about Jesus with our friends, family and people at school. We share Jesus every day through our attitudes, actions, and words. Later in the New Testament, Paul says to Christ-followers in Corinth:

You yourselves are our letter, written on our hearts, known and read by everyone. You show that you are a letter from Christ, the result of our ministry, written not with ink but with the Spirit of the living God, not on tablets of stone but on tablets of human hearts. — 2 Corinthians 3:2-3

 *(talk)*

Pretend you are with some friends who start talking about God.
Read their viewpoints and follow the instructions below.

TJ

I don't think the writers of the Bible were as concerned
about every detail as we are today. Actually, I don't
understand why some Christians think they have to prove
the Bible has no contradicting stories. It actually makes
people not want to be Christians. Smart people won't
believe in God if they are forced to think some accounts
don't actually contradict when they clearly do.

WRITE A QUESTION YOU'D LIKE TO ASK TJ:

_____

JESS

It's really important that every detail is correct in the
Bible. God inspired it. Even if the authors of the Bible
weren't worried about all the little details, God still
helped them get it all right. The things that look like
errors are not really errors at all. You can explain each
of them pretty easily.

WRITE A QUESTION YOU'D LIKE TO ASK JESS:

_____

WILL

If the Bible has contradictions in it, how can you trust anything it says? If the writers have different stories about Jesus' resurrection, how do we know that it actually happened at all? It's popular right now to unfairly question the Bible. If you don't accept every word of the Bible as directly perfect from God, how can you be a Christian?

WRITE A QUESTION YOU'D LIKE TO ASK WILL:

_____

JULIE

Some Christians try to harmonize all the mistakes in the Bible. They take two different stories and they try to say they fit together somehow. Jesus' resurrection is an example. Don't try and make a story so that the different accounts all magically work together. Just admit they are different. It doesn't mean Jesus didn't rise from the dead.

WRITE A QUESTION YOU'D LIKE TO ASK JULIE:

_____

Talk with your group about why you asked the questions you wrote down above.

What other questions does this study raise for you about the Bible?

Session

3

Can I be a Christian and believe in evolution?

Big Idea

Students will wrestle with tough questions about biblical interpretation, coming to terms with their answers' ramifications for the relationship between science and faith.

You'll Need

In *(leader notes)*

— — — — — — — — — — — —

⊗ Your copy of this Leader Guide and a Student Guide for each participant.

⊗ To explore ahead of time your church/denomination's take on evolution specifically, and the relationship of scripture and science more generally. Later in the session you will be asked to articulate this to students.

⊗ A pencil or pen for each participant.

Tom couldn't sleep.

He kept replaying in his mind a conversation from his biology class earlier in the day. The topic was evolution, and he ended up becoming the center of attention.

"Evolution does not match up with the Bible." Mrs. Bronson had repeated that phrase at least five times during class that day. Tom liked Mrs. Bronson, but it was clear she didn't believe in God. "As a scientist and historian, I must inform you that that the Bible's version of how the world began is incompatible with science."

Mrs. Bronson split the class into groups to discuss Charles Darwin and evolutionary theories. Most people in Tom's high school knew he went to church. As soon as Tom got into his group with five other students, the questions began:

"You don't believe in evolution, do you Tom?"

"Sorry, but isn't it kind of ignorant to think the Bible is true when science so clearly contradicts the Bible?"

Tom didn't know what to say. He felt embarrassed and childish when the other students kept insisting science made faith in God irrelevant.

The irony is that Tom actually believed evolution *could* be true, but he believed God is real too. He was ashamed to admit his belief in evolution *and* God because his girlfriend, Jen, had a strong opinion about that.

"You can't believe in both evolution and God," Jen said. "The Bible says God created the world in six days and then rested."

"But couldn't it have been longer than six 24-hour periods?" Tom asked. He went back and read chapters one and two of Genesis. Tom wondered whether or not this was actually supposed to be a scientific account of creation.

"Why are you doubting God?" Jen replied. "You should have faith that what the Bible says is actually true. If you don't believe Genesis is true and that God did what it says in that book, how do you know that Jesus isn't just a fake story too?"

These conversations kept Tom awake at night. He started to wonder, *"If I believe in evolution and science, can I still be a Christian?"*

(questions)

> Have you ever experienced anything like the story above?

 (leader notes)

Many teenagers struggle with the cultural dynamic that pits religion against science. The media often portrays a dichotomy: either the Bible is true or science is true. In fact, this might be what your church or ministry organization teaches as well. Again, make sure you create an environment where students feel free to express their own thoughts before you share your own.

In the beginning God created the heavens and the earth. Now the earth was formless and empty, darkness was over the surface of the deep, and the Spirit of God was hovering over the waters.

And God said, "Let there be light," and there was light. God saw that the light was good, and he separated the light from the darkness. God called the light "day," and the darkness he called "night." And there was evening, and there was morning—the first day.

— Genesis 1:1-5

Thus the heavens and the earth were completed in all their vast array.

By the seventh day God had finished the work he had been doing; so on the seventh day he rested from all his work. Then God blessed the seventh day and made it holy, because on it he rested from all the work of creating that he had done.

— Genesis 2:1-3

What do *you* think of the creation stories in Genesis 1 and 2? Are they written as precise historical accounts, poetic stories about how God created all things, or something else? Why do you think that?

(leader notes)

We are moving toward helping students understand the idea of biblical "genre." Explore the idea of whether or not every word of the Bible should be taken literally. The key question here is, "What kind of genre is Genesis 1 and 2?" This is a critical question in the "science versus faith" debate. If Genesis 1-2 is scientific in its genre, there is a major conflict between modern science and the Christian faith. If Genesis 1-2 is poetic in genre, there may be less conflict regarding faith and science. Or, it might be that the passage is a *poem* that *describes* scientific history, in which case both "sides" of this debate have some merit!

> Tom wondered, *can you be a Christian and believe in evolution?* What do you think of that question?

 (leader notes)

Let them talk, careful not to share your opinion just yet. If you give your "answer" up front, it is highly likely the conversation will not move any deeper than your opinion. This study is written in a way that acknowledges different churches and traditions will answer this question very differently. We also have a hunch that different high school students within all those traditions are wrestling to articulate responses they believe to be true. You get to serve as a guide to listen and facilitate dialogue.

> What does your church believe about this
> question? If you don't know ... take a guess.

 (*leader notes*)

This should be interesting data for you. What are the
students of your church or ministry hearing about
this topic and from where? What can you do with this
information?

Study up ahead of time on your church and/or tradition's
take on this issue, and share it here.

(notes)

 (leader notes)

— — — — — — — — — — — — —

Have your group take turns reading this section out loud. Ask for thoughts after each person reads, and feel free to add your own insights. You don't have to stay in this section long.

Understanding "Biblical Interpretation"

Different people read or interpret the Bible in different ways. "Hermeneutics" (pronounced herm – uh – NOO – ticks … say it a few times fast … it's fun) is a fancy word for this. Interpretation is like the "lens" through which you read the Bible. We've already explored this process some in the last session.

Imagine taking a picture with a camera or your phone. The setting or filter you use can change how the picture looks—sometimes dramatically. Similarly, your experiences can affect your interpretation or "biblical hermeneutic." Everyone (even you!) has a hermeneutic. Your life has influenced you to read the Bible from a certain perspective. That's not a good or bad thing; it's just reality. And it's something to pay attention to as you read.

Ok, that's nice... But what does hermeneutics have to do with evolution?

Literal and Figurative Interpretation of the Bible

Some people use a "literal interpretation" approach to scripture. A literal interpretation means Genesis 1 tells us the world was created in seven 24-hour periods.

"Figurative interpretation" takes the approach that some stories in the Bible may not be based on real historical events. They are stories that were created to make a point or tell a story, like Jesus' use of parables. A figurative interpretation of Genesis 1 might see it as a poetic story of God's creation of the world that was never intended to be scientifically accurate.

Christians Have Different Opinions on Biblical Interpretation

C.S. Lewis, who wrote the *Chronicles of Narnia* and some books on theology, believed not all biblical passages were meant to be literal. Some people in his day read the book of Revelation and were nervous that heaven would be boring. To that worry, Lewis wrote:

"... if they cannot understand books written for grown-ups, they should not talk about them. All the Scriptural imagery (harps, crowns, gold, etc.) is, of course, a merely symbolical attempt to express the inexpressible." [8]

Which approach do you tend to take – literal or figurative? Can you use both approaches to scripture? How?

Why do you think Lewis would make such a strong statement about interpreting the Bible?

John MacArthur, a well-known current-day pastor, believes in a more literal approach to reading scripture:

"Everything Scripture teaches about sin and redemption assumes the literal truth of the first three chapters of Genesis. If we wobble to any degree on the truth of this passage, we undermine the very foundations of our faith." [9]

> Why does MacArthur say a literal approach to Genesis 1-3 is so important?

 (leader notes)

You might note that according to MacArthur's argument here, our theological understanding of sin is undermined if Genesis 3 is not read literally. Others may argue a literal interpretation is not required in order to arrive at the same understanding of sin's origin.

CONTEXT!

The ancient Biblical writers were a mix of poets, prophets, and historians. Therefore, some people believe their accounts of the beginning of the world—while inspired by God—were not meant to be taken *scientifically*.

Others disagree. They say God inspired the writers to know more than was humanly possible about what happened in the creation events. Their creation account is taken literally because it is directly from God. Even if they weren't trained scientists or even personally observed what they were writing about, God inspired them and all the details are scientifically accurate.

S *(scripture)*

Even though there are differences between how people read the Bible, almost everyone agrees that not *every* word in the Bible is literal. For example, Jesus used many stories and examples to help make a point. The following passage is Jesus warning his followers about the danger of sin and how seriously we should treat things that pull us away from God:

> *If your hand or your foot gets in God's way, chop it off and throw it away. You're better off maimed or lame and alive than the proud owner of two hands and two feet, godless in a furnace of eternal fire. And if your eye distracts you from God, pull it out and throw it away. You're better off one-eyed and alive than exercising your twenty-twenty vision from inside the fire of hell.*
>
> —Mark 9:43-48, The Message

WARNING: PLEASE DO NOT TAKE THE SCRIPTURE ABOVE 100% LITERALLY.

How many hands and eyes would you have if you took Jesus' command literally? I'm pretty sure you'd be left without hands, feet, or eyes. But don't worry—so would everyone else!

What do you think is Jesus' main point in this passage?

How does this relate to what we have been talking about?

 In *(leader notes)*

This is a *key* moment of the study. Jesus' main point is not to spread a philosophy of self-mutilation. Jesus' point is to help his followers understand the severity of the problem of sin. Taking this passage literally could be a bad idea. Jesus used hyperbole to get his point across, sort of like saying you'd give "an arm and a leg" to get a new cell phone. We need to identify this literary device in order to interpret Jesus' words. Note that Jesus is still presenting a hard teaching here. He's using strong language to get an important point across.

In *(leader notes)*

— — — — — — — — — — — —

After your group identifies the main point of this passage, ask them to identify the main point of Genesis 1 and 2. Apart from a person's opinion on how literal to take this creation narrative, one of the main goals of Genesis 1 and 2 seems to be *to describe the relationship between God, creation, and human beings.* In Genesis 1 and 2 we learn that:

1. God is present and involved in creation.

2. God creates all things and calls them "good."

3. God creates human beings in God's image and calls them "very good."

4. Human beings are given a role in creation: to multiply and to care for the world God made.

5. Genesis 3 expands our understanding by showing humanity's rebellion against God as sin enters the world.

NOTE: Just to share a bit of our bias here, we're convinced that students could spend a lifetime debating whether Genesis 1 and 2 is scientific history, poem, or something else, and miss the point of this rich description of God's desire and design for relationship with us. Interpretation is important, but sometimes our debates about interpretation can cloud our vision of who God is and what God is up to in our lives and the world. You can decide based on your own tradition and interpretive lens whether to include a comment to this end in your discussion.

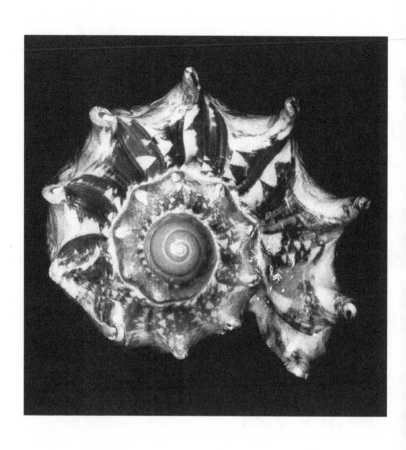

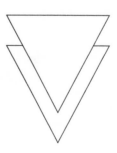

(talk)

Pretend you are with some friends who start talking about God. Read their viewpoints and follow the instructions below.

ABBY

I think the Bible should be read literally. If you don't read it for what it says, then how can someone determine what is true and what is just story? It seems to me if you don't think everything is literal, Jesus could just be a made-up story too. I think you need to take the Bible either "all or nothing." That's what faith is: trusting God's word to be true, because God says it's true.

FERNANDO

I don't understand why the Bible has to be taken literally at all. The writers of the Bible are writing fictional stories with a point. Just because those stories didn't happen doesn't mean the point isn't still the same. The story of Jonah doesn't need to be true for me to believe the point of the story: we need to love people who don't love us.

BRETT

The Bible is something that takes effort and clear thinking to really understand. Some passages should be taken literally and others can be taken as more of a story. I believe that Jesus was a real person, but I don't believe that Genesis 1-3 is a literal story. Some stories in the Bible sound like real stories to me, but others sound like they were invented to make a good point. I'd rather focus on what the point of the story is than argue over whether it really happened or not.

JANELLE

I struggle to believe things that can't be verified by science. How can we know any of the stories and characters in the Bible to be true since we can't scientifically verify that they happened? I know a lot of Christians and think a lot of them are good people, but it doesn't make sense to me that they would base their lives on a book that is full of ancient stories with no science to back them up.

Which of these opinions is closest to yours?

Which of these opinions is furthest from yours? Why?

What is the best point each person makes?

 (leader notes)

After your group responds to this question, this is a great opportunity for you to share your own thoughts on this topic if you haven't already.

Do you think the Bible should be read more literally or figuratively? Place an "X" on the line below to indicate where you stand right now. The left side is very literal. The right side is more figurative. Or you might feel like you're somewhere in the middle.

Literal   *Figurative*

Why did you put your X where you did?

 (leader notes)

This is actually a bit of a trick question to get them talking. It is not ideal to simply apply an overarching "literal or figurative" interpretation to the entire Bible. So after students explain why they put their "X" where they did, you might try to explore the question of "genres" that are evident in various parts of the Bible.

Let your students know that when they are reading scripture, they can ask, "Is this particular book or passage meant by the author to be poetry? Allegory? Historical account? Pastoral letter? Wisdom? If I'm not sure, how could I find out?" The type of writing employed will help a reader determine which frames to use to interpret the passage.

Bring the conversation full circle by helping students see that some people view the beginning of Genesis as a poetic genre, while others see it as a scientific historical account. We will never know the full story about the original creation until all creation is made new by God, so make sure students know it's okay to walk away from this discussion with some unresolved tension. That will be true of most of the following sessions as well as this study addresses more controversial issues.

Are there any other questions you have about this topic right now? Write them here, and if you're willing, share them with the group.

Session

4   Does God discriminate against women?

Big Idea

Students will gain a basic understanding of the complex issues involved in developing biblical views of women in leadership in both the church and home. This session will help some students understand why this is an important question, even if they don't fully arrive at answers.

You'll Need

 (leader notes)

⊗ Your copy of this Leader Guide and a Student Guide for each participant.

⊗ A pencil or pen for each participant.

⊗ To read this study ahead of time, as well as additional scripture passages: 1 Corinthians 14:33-35, Ephesians 5:21-33, and 1 Corinthians 11:3.

⊗ To learn more about your own church and denominational tradition's positions on women in leadership in the church and the home. Also think about actual practices within your tradition and your church (sometimes these are different from the stated positions) and how students might call those out and want to discuss them.

Dawn's friend Ty invited her to Sunday morning church.

Dawn decided to go, though she was way more interested in Ty than in the service itself.

But the morning surprised Dawn. Instead of a worship service with music and a talk, it was a meeting where the church was voting on the decision to hire a new pastor. Now that seemed like no big deal, but *everyone* was angry. People were yelling into a microphone about the new pastor and some were furious that the church was going to hire this person. Then Dawn found out why there was so much controversy.

The new pastor was a woman.

One person walked up to the microphone with a Bible in hand and said:

"How can we possibly be choosing a woman as our pastor? The Bible is clear that women should not be allowed to lead in that kind of role. 1 Timothy 2:11-14 says, 'A woman should learn in quietness and full submission. I do not permit a woman to teach or to assume authority over a man; she must be quiet. For Adam was formed first, then Eve. And Adam was not the one deceived; it was the woman who was deceived and became a sinner.'"

Dawn was shocked. Women can't teach? They're supposed to keep silent? She had no idea that passage was in the Bible. She wondered, *"Does being a Christian mean that I have to believe women are somehow inferior to men?"*

She decided to ask Ty about it.

"Women should let men lead," Ty replied. "I think that's not only true for church, but for families, too. The Bible says it clearly, and that's how our family works. My mom has never complained about it."

Dawn was confused. She didn't know she had to believe this in order to be a Christian.

 (*questions*)

> Did you know the Bible has passages like the one quoted in our story? What do you know about those passages?

 (*leader notes*)

Many of the teenagers we worked with in piloting this curriculum had never heard some of the relevant scriptural passages regarding gender and leadership. Listen to what your students have to say so you can judge their previous knowledge and engagement with this topic.

There are two areas of gender leadership discussed in this study:

1. How does scripture view men and women with regard to leadership in the church?

2. How does scripture view men and women with regard to leadership in the relationships in a family unit?

Consider reading other passages to help your group explore this topic, such as 1 Corinthians 14:33-35, Ephesians 5:21-33, or 1 Corinthians 11:3.

> What is your opinion NOW (before you go further in this study)? Do you think women should be allowed to serve in the church? What about in marriage and in the family? Why?

 (leader notes)

Listen for their opinions and response. Again, resist the temptation to fully direct the conversation by sharing your opinion just yet!

> How much does this issue matter to you personally? Scale from 1-10?
> 1 = very little, 10 = LOTS! Why?

 (leader notes)

For some teenagers, this may be the number one issue that troubles them regarding faith. For others, they may have never even considered it before. This is a great exercise to help those who don't really care about this topic hear from their peers who do. Assigning a number to their answer ("scale from 1-10" above) is a great technique for any small group discussion because it is an unthreatening way for people to share their opinion without having to use words (which can be challenging for some teenagers).

> What does your church believe about women in leadership in the church or in marriage? If you don't know, take a guess!

 (leader notes)

One of the reasons we ask this question is to make sure you, as a leader, know the answer to this question as well. If you're a volunteer, be sure to talk to your church or organizational leadership to understand how this issue is approached. Thoughtful churches and organizations often have different opinions about this topic even when they agree on many others.

 *(notes)*

CONTEXT!

It is important to know how women were treated during the time the New Testament was written, especially within Ancient Near Eastern culture. In general, women were not considered equal to men. For example, women were typically:

* Forbidden to talk to men (except their husbands)

* Not allowed to worship with men

* Forced to cover their heads, because hair was considered private

* Restricted to household work only

* Not considered reliable witnesses in a court of law

> Okay... How does all of this context affect how I read the Bible when it comes to women and men in leadership?

BONUS CONTEXT! (Lucky you...)

Some scholars believe Paul, who wrote the letter of 1 Timothy quoted in the opening story, intended this instruction specifically for Timothy and the people in Ephesus (the city where Timothy lived), but it is not necessarily meant for all places and all times. This position suggests that Paul was nervous that if women broke too many social norms (like teaching), people would reject Christianity—not because of Jesus, but because of the early church's countercultural view of women.

Other scholars and leaders believe Paul's words rise above a particular context and apply across cultures and centuries, much like the words of Jesus throughout the gospels. This is part of a bigger question about what in the Bible should be read as a "timeless truth" and what should be read as a teaching meant for a specific time, place, and people—or if there are such distinctions in scripture.

The Genesis Argument

The passage from 1 Timothy 2 in the opening story argues that Eve sinned first and therefore no woman should have authority over a man. This is sometimes called "The Genesis Argument." Here are two possible views Christians hold toward these verses:

1. *Women should not lead men:* Because 1 Timothy 2 refers to Genesis, many Christians believe this passage is not only relevant to Timothy and the Ephesians. The reference to Eve should be read as a general statement about all women. Therefore, it applies to our lives today.

2. *Women should be able to lead men:* Genesis shows that women carry out many of the same duties as men. For example, both women and men were asked to care for the garden, and both genders were created in the image of God with no apparent initial leadership differences. Therefore, women can be called by God to lead groups or churches that include men.

Church Leadership: Two BIG words

Complementarians generally believe men are the spiritual leaders of the church. Women can play important roles, but not lead men.

Egalitarians generally believe men and women are equal in the church, and members from either gender can lead.

It's important to note that many church traditions and individual believers fall somewhere between these big-worded positions. For example, a church or denomination might encourage women to lead certain ministries or even a church board, but not become ordained pastors. Or perhaps women can serve as associate pastors, but not as senior pastors.

> If our society has changed a lot in the way we view women, should the church adapt too?

 In *(leader notes)*

This is a great opportunity to explore the purpose of the church and its role in culture. If the church is primarily the embodiment of Christ in the world (e.g., Romans 12:3-8, 1 Corinthians 12:12-27, and similar passages), we live as an alternative community proclaiming good news with our words and way of life.

Wonder aloud with your students about how culture impacts the church, and how the church impacts culture. What does it mean to be "a chosen people, a royal priesthood, a holy nation, God's special possession, that you may declare the praises of him who called you out of darkness into his wonderful light" (1 Peter 2:9) while also becoming "all things to all people so that by all possible means" some might be saved (1 Corinthians 9:22)?

Examples of Women Leading in the Bible

Egalitarians might argue that, despite passages like 1 Timothy 2, there are also several examples in scripture of women showing leadership of various kinds. Here are some of those passages:

* *Miriam (Exodus 15)*
* *Deborah (Judges 4-5)*
* *Huldah* (2 Kings 22)
* *Anna (Luke 2)*
* *Priscilla* (Acts 18)
* *Phoebe, Junia, and others (Romans 16)*

Now what about women and men in marriage and family relationships?

Home Leadership: Head and Helper or Equal Partners?

Some Christians believe God designed men and women with equal value but to play different roles, in particular in the husband-wife relationship and the leadership of the family overall.

This view holds that the husband's calling from God takes priority in life decisions and wives should support and help fulfill those decisions. For example, read Ephesians 5:22-23:

Wives, submit yourselves to your own husbands as you do to the Lord. For the husband is the head of the wife as Christ is the head of the church, his body, of which he is the Savior.

Other Christians think husbands and wives can have more egalitarian relationships in the home, dividing roles more according to gifts and skills, and making decisions together. Some of these folks might point to Ephesians 5 as well, but look more at verse 21 as the context for the rest: "Submit to one another out of reverence for Christ."

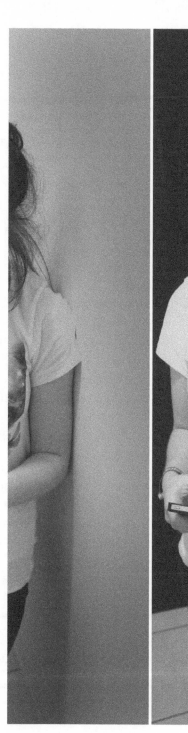

S *(scripture)*

In *(leader notes)*

— — — — — — — — — — — — —

The story below is an interesting passage that may sound different when we read it in the light of its cultural context. Some say that Jesus' acceptance of this woman makes an important comment on his view of women versus the view of women in the culture of his day. Whether your church follows a more complementarian or egalitarian view of women and men in leadership, this passage can help affirm the value women have as persons created and loved by God, and their value as part of the church.

It's important when you read a passage to get a sense of what the whole Bible says about that topic rather than make judgments based on only one verse or passage of scripture. The Bible may have things to say about that topic elsewhere too.

> **WARNING: DON'T LET ONE VERSE SPEAK FOR THE WHOLE BIBLE**

In *(leader notes)*

— — — — — — — — — — — —

We like to share this saying with high schoolers: *"A text without a context is a pretext"* and then ask them to explain it. The phrase means that interpreting a passage of scripture by itself without understanding its background or purpose within the text is a dangerous way to make claims about the meaning of scripture as a whole.

Help students understand that using one verse isolated from context and failing to seek the entire wisdom of the scriptures can be dangerous. Sometimes bad doctrines are built on reading a text in isolation.

It's *always* a good idea to see what Jesus thought and did about something. Read the passage on the next page describing a woman who finds out Jesus is nearby and comes to see him. As you read it, think about parts of the story where you wonder if Jesus breaks a "cultural rule."

In *(leader notes)*

— — — — — — — — — — — —

Invite someone to read the passage out loud, then ask what rules students think Jesus might have been breaking.

A woman in that town who lived a sinful life learned that Jesus was eating at the Pharisee's house, so she came there with an alabaster jar of perfume. As she stood behind him at his feet weeping, she began to wet his feet with her tears. Then she wiped them with her hair, kissed them and poured perfume on them.

When the Pharisee who had invited him saw this, he said to himself, "If this man were a prophet, he would know who is touching him and what kind of woman she is—that she is a sinner."

Jesus answered him, "Simon, I have something to tell you."

"Tell me, teacher," he said.

"Two people owed money to a certain moneylender. One owed him five hundred denarii, and the other fifty. Neither of them had the money to pay him back, so he forgave the debts of both. Now which of them will love him more?"

Simon replied, "I suppose the one who had the bigger debt forgiven."

"You have judged correctly," Jesus said.

Then he turned toward the woman and said to Simon, "Do you see this woman? I came into your house. You did not give me any water for my feet, but she wet my feet with her tears and wiped them with her hair. You did not give me a kiss, but this woman, from the time I entered, has not stopped kissing my feet. You did not put oil on my head, but she has poured perfume on my feet. Therefore, I tell you, her many sins have been forgiven—as her great love has shown. But whoever has been forgiven little loves little."

Then Jesus said to her, "Your sins are forgiven."

The other guests began to say among themselves, "Who is this who even forgives sins?"

Jesus said to the woman, "Your faith has saved you; go in peace."

— Luke 7:37-50

These quick notes of context may help:

* A woman labeled "sinner" was likely a prostitute or adulterer.

* If someone talked to a "sinner," that person was considered "unclean," meaning they couldn't participate in religious gatherings or rituals.

* The Pharisees were the ultra-religious types who wanted to make sure religious laws were never broken.

* Women often did not even speak in the presence of men in any public place.

* Feet were considered one of the dirtiest parts of a person. It was unusual to touch another's feet.

* Women's hair was considered private, even sexual.

In *(leader notes)*

Don't assume every teenager knows the definitions
of prostitution and adultery.

In *(leader notes)*

— — — — — —   — — — — — —

As you process the questions below with your group, you might keep in mind these points as well:

1) This passage does NOT specifically address women's roles in the church or home, so we need to be careful in using this story to directly support a particular view.

2) This passage does show Jesus treating this woman in a way that could be considered equal to any other person, even in a shockingly radical way. (For further study of this story and its implications, consider reading Kenneth Bailey's *Jesus Through Middle Eastern Eyes*.) But if you aren't inclined to go that far, consider how the passage might affirm that Jesus was willing to care for and offer healing and salvation to both women and men, even when it was scandalous to do so.

How does Jesus surprise you in this passage?

How does this passage speak to Jesus' view of the value of this woman?

> What other biblical passages affect our understanding of women's value in God's eyes?

> What about passages that say something about women in leadership or in family relationships?

In (leader notes)

It's unlikely that students will know other relevant scripture you might want to explore. So here are a few passages for discussion depending on how much time you have:

Galatians 3:28: *"There is neither Jew nor Gentile, neither slave nor free, nor is there male and female, for you are all one in Christ Jesus."*

Some scholars call this the first-ever written statement of equality in human history. This is sometimes used as a text for an egalitarian view of women in leadership and/ or the family. But it can also simply be an affirmation that assigning gender roles does not change anyone's inherent value.

1 Corinthians 14:34: *"Women should remain silent in the churches. They are not allowed to speak, but must be in submission, as the law says."*

Some scholars believe that this prohibition of women speaking or teaching in church still holds true today.

t (*talk*)

Take a moment to pretend you are at college, or in the military, or at your job and are with some of your new friends who start talking about God. Read the viewpoints below and follow the instructions.

Mark if you agree, $\ominus$ if you do not agree, and $\bigcirc$ for neutral.

SAM

I don't think women should be angry about not being allowed to lead in the church. They have a different role to play that is just as important. It's just not leadership. If both women and men could accept the roles that God has created for them, the church would be better off.

JILL

I hate that the Bible says women shouldn't lead in the church, but the Bible is what I follow, even if I don't like it. Even though I'm gifted in leading, I won't do it because I trust the Bible. Sometimes there are things in the Bible that we don't understand, but we have to trust God because God has a better perspective than we do.

In (*leader notes*)

— — — — — — — — — — — — — —

Jill's point is worth dwelling on. What happens when we read something in the Bible that we don't agree with? Jill's tensions raise important questions regarding biblical interpretation and the authority of scripture in the life of the believer.

MIGUEL

The Bible actually is one of the most liberating books ever for women. The way Jesus treated women totally gave them more freedom. There are many passages where women are given positions of leadership and the Bible makes it clear they are equal to men. The passages that seem not to allow women in leadership were actually just written for the first century context. They don't apply to us today.

KARIN

I think the Bible is wrong in its stance on women. There are some things written in the Bible that I can't accept. I know some people say that we should accept everything the Bible says, but in this case, I don't think it's right to agree with the Bible. Passages like the one in 1 Timothy have been used to harm women for years. No matter what the Bible says, I refuse to agree with it if it hurts someone.

You should have circled one of the three buttons after each person above. Why did you choose the button you chose?

> One more thing I'd like to say about this topic is ...

 (leader notes)

Depending on how your session ends, you may want to ask your group for brief thoughts on the next session's topic.

Is Jesus really the only way to God?

Session

5

Big Idea

Students will explore the claim that Jesus Christ is the only, unique way to life with God.

You'll Need

In *(leader notes)*

⊗ Your copy of this Leader Guide and a Student Guide for each participant.

⊗ A pencil or pen for each participant.

⊗ To read this study ahead of time. Note that in this session our bias toward the uniqueness of Jesus Christ and the Christian faith comes through, especially in the Leader Notes. We're guessing most of the leaders who utilize this curriculum will lean in this direction, but the goal is still to help students engage with other sides to this claim. Another goal is to help them develop a sense of respect for people who hold different views even while they pursue their own commitment to Jesus.

Jamal and Chris had always been friends, but their arguments were getting personal.

"I feel like you're saying that I am going to hell," Chris said with anger. His conversations with Jamal about God had been light-hearted up until now, but Chris was tired of Jamal making him feel like his Mormon faith was inadequate.

"I'm sorry, but I think Mormonism is wrong, Chris," Jamal answered. "And it's not for me to decide who is going to heaven and who is going to hell—only God does that. But I believe that the only people who will be with God forever are those who believe Jesus is Lord."

"But I do believe in Jesus," Chris responded.

"Not the same way that I do," Jamal replied.

Chris and Jamal decided not to talk to each other for a couple of days. When they saw each other again, it was over lunch with some other friends. Susannah, who claimed to be "kinda Jewish," joined in the conversation.

"I don't understand why you're arguing about which religion is better," Susannah said. "The only thing that matters is that you believe in some version of God and be a loving person. All religions are basically the same idea but with different names."

"I agree with Susannah," Martin added as he plopped down beside them with his lunch. "This is exactly why the world will never have peace. Religious fights will never help us get along with each other."

Jamal had heard at his church that he needed to be committed to Jesus and Jesus alone. But he didn't know how to respond to Chris, Susannah or Martin.

How should I think about my friends' faith? he wondered to himself. *Am I being too closed-minded about religion?*

(*questions*)

Have you ever been part of a story like this?
What happened?

  (*leader notes*)

If you have a story to share about a time when you were in the kind of conversation described above, you might also share that with the group.

If not, or if students bring it up, the commonly-seen "Coexist" symbol on the next page represents a blend of religous symbols.

What do you think of Susannah's and Martin's comments in this story? Who do you agree or disagree with more? What would you say?

 (leader notes)

Try to get your group to respond to the idea that the only thing that matters is to "be a good person." One way to ask this question is to say, **"Are people born basically good? Or are people born with selfishness that can lead to evil?"** Most teenagers have discussed that question in a high school class already, so it will be relevant to them.

The ideology that religion is a moral system designed to make us good people conflicts with the Bible's claim that we are all tainted by sin and need rescuing. This rescue comes in the form of Jesus Christ. The question about whether we can just try hard and make ourselves good or we are in need of rescue points to the heart of the gospel.

What do you think of the way Jamal handled himself in this story?

How do you think Jamal is doing when it comes to sharing his faith with "gentleness and respect" (1 Peter 3:15-16)? How important do you think that is?

How were you raised in your family to think about salvation and the difference among religious faiths?

What does your church believe about salvation and the difference among religious faiths?

 *(notes)*

In *(leader notes)*

— — — — — — — — — — — —

A major goal in the following section is to get your group to recognize there *are* significant differences among world religions. On key central points about the identity of Jesus Christ, they disagree. The Christian gospel says a specific, real human being (who was God in the flesh) named Jesus entered our world for the purpose of reconciling all humanity and creation to God. This chart shows some of the ways other faiths think and talk about Jesus.

> **Do all religions see Jesus the same?** Here is a table showing different viewpoints about Jesus' identity, purpose, and resurrection from the dead. These are only a few of the world's religious traditions, but ones you might have come across in the U.S. or your own community.

Religious Tradition	Christianity	Islam	Judaism	Buddhism	Mormonism
Who was Jesus?	Both God and human. As part of the Trinity, he is the savior of human beings.	A human being who was a prophet of God, but not as great as the prophet Muhammad.	A human being, but not the Messiah (King, or Savior) Jews are waiting for.	A good person, but not God. There is no "God."	He was a human being at first, but later he became a god.
Why did he come?	To rescue human beings from sin by the gift of grace, to show us how to live in right relationship with God & the world.	He came to show God's (Allah's) will for people.	A rabbi who falsely claimed to be the Messiah & fulfill scripture. Jesus not mentioned in any sacred texts.	Jesus came to help people who need enlightenment.	A god & example for us. Human beings may also attain the status of being a god by following Jesus' example of love & sacrifice.
Was Jesus resurrected from the dead?	Yes.	No.	No.	No. Buddhists believe in reincarnation, or coming to life as another being after death.	Yes.

Which differences in the religions listed in the diagram do you think are most important?

Word to know: *Religious Pluralism* is the belief that all religions are equally valid. Religious pluralists believe that even though some religions might contradict each other, each holds a part of the eternal truth of the Divine.

John Hick, a well-known proponent of religious pluralism, teaches, "Applying a kind of philosophical Golden Rule, it would be unreasonable not to grant to religious experience within other traditions what I affirm of it within my own tradition."

 (leader notes)

Students may not know the term "Golden Rule," but it is a reference to a culturally-accepted adaptation of Matthew 7:12, "Do to others what you would have them do to you." Hick uses this as a way to say that all religions need to completely respect the rights of other religions to be equally valid. Hick's viewpoint is one of the most common ways to think about religion today in our culture.

Wonder aloud with students whether it's possible to treat respectfully people who hold different beliefs, while stopping short of seeing those beliefs as equal with the claims of Christianity.

Are Christians "Narrow Minded"?

Tim Keller, pastor of Redeemer Presbyterian Church in New York City, writes, "It is no more narrow to claim that one religion is right than to claim that one way to think about all religions (namely that all are equal) is right." Keller is saying that any stance we take—whether it's Christianity or religious pluralism—inherently prefers one perspective over others. In other words, there's nothing essentially "narrow minded" about believing that Jesus is the only way to God.

Do we have a "jealous" God?

Read Exodus 20:4-6 and the story in Exodus 32:1-14.

> Why would God ever be "jealous"?

 In *(leader notes)*

If you decide to dwell here, encourage your group to wonder whether God's jealousy could be positive. In this case, God is angry that Israel is worshiping a golden calf. Perhaps God's anger is ultimately motivated by love. God knows worship of anything other than God is actually harmful to us.

S   *(scripture)*

One of the most radical claims Jesus made comes from John 14. As Jesus is talking to his disciples and is preparing to be killed and then rise again from the dead, he says:

"Do not let your hearts be troubled. You believe in God; believe also in me. My Father's house has many rooms; if that were not so, would I have told you that I am going there to prepare a place for you? And if I go and prepare a place for you, I will come back and take you to be with me that you also may be where I am. You know the way to the place where I am going."

Thomas said to him, "Lord, we don't know where you are going, so how can we know the way?"

Jesus answered, "I am the way and the truth and the life. No one comes to the Father except through me. If you really know me, you will know my Father as well. From now on, you do know him and have seen him."

— John 14:1-7

What does Jesus mean when he says he is the "Way"? the "Truth"? the "Life"?

In *(leader notes)*

Help students grasp the audacity of this comment. Verses 4 and 5 talk about "the way" to where Jesus is going. In verse 6, Jesus claims, "I am the way." A "way" links two things together. Jesus is the link between sinful human beings and a holy God. What are some other implications of Jesus claiming to be the Way?

"Truth" – Jesus is making a statement that he is totally reliable. Everything he has taught and done is trustworthy. He embodies God's truth.

"Life" – This is an amazing word coming from someone who would die a few hours later. Jesus seems to say that there is far more to life than what we experience now. To follow Jesus (the way) and trust him (truth) leads us to life: real life in the present as well as eternal life with God and resurrection from the dead.

> Underline what is said in the previous passage that might impact how we view religious pluralism.

 (leader notes)

"No one comes to the Father except through me" is the primary statement of importance. Jesus is not saying that by learning from him or following his example, people can know God more. As one theologian notes, "Jesus does not merely point the way, *he is the Way*." [10]

Never in the Bible do we see evidence for God's tolerance of worshiping other things or gods as helping human beings develop a strong relationship with God. God is always opposed to it. It is not the way we were designed to flourish.

> If there were other ways for human beings to be in a right relationship with God, why did Jesus die on a cross?

 (leader notes)

In Galatians 2, Paul makes the argument that no one can be made right with God merely by following the Jewish law. Paul goes on to teach, "I do not nullify the grace of God; for if justification comes through the law, then Christ died for nothing" (2:21). While Paul is referring specifically to the observance of religious law, an argument can be made that substituting *anything* else for Jesus means that he died for nothing, since it wouldn't have been necessary. In other words, if being right with God can come through anything other than Jesus, the death of Jesus Christ is an unnecessary sacrifice.

> Respond to this statement: "Religious pluralism destroys the personality of God."

 (leader notes)

Some of your more intellectual kids will appreciate this comment. Let them try to respond to it before you explain that if all faiths are the same, we are not treating God as if God is a being that has a "unique personality."

If the gospel of Jesus is true, that means we have a God who is incredibly gracious and forgiving. Our God's "personality" is such that God will even go to the length of dying personally for our reconciliation to God and to one another.

That is a different "personality" than some faith systems that believe God instead requires human beings to earn their righteousness. Those are two different "God personalities." Ultimately, since Christianity believes God values relationships at the core, the personality of God is actually quite important.

What do you think Jesus means in Revelation 21:5 when he says, "I am making everything new"? If Jesus' mission is to restore all things, how do we live in a way that points to that kind of hope?

 (leader notes)

The hope is to end this conversation with a reminder that our daily lives reflect not only "what happens after we die" kind of faith, but a faith that gets lived out here and now. Jesus' life, death, and resurrection have all kinds of implications for life on this earth in these bodies and this particular time and place.

 *(talk)*

Pretend you are with some friends who start talking about God.
Read their viewpoints and follow the instructions below.

ELI

Faith is a personal thing. I will always respect what you
believe. All I'm asking for in return is that you respect
what I believe. To say that my religious beliefs are false
is intolerant. I think Jesus is a wonderful example, but
there are other ways to find great truth too. We should
affirm each other's belief in God and stick together so we
can bring good to the world.

CARLA

Jesus is the center of my life and faith. I'm not concerned
about getting into arguments with people, but I do believe
Jesus is the true way to know God. Jesus told us to make
disciples, so I will spend my life trying to help other
people know him. People will know Jesus by the way I love
others and it's important to share Jesus whenever I can so
that everyone can know the truth.

SCOTT

We need to fight for Jesus in today's world. Everyone is
so afraid of offending other people that we lose a sense
of what makes us different and unique. Christianity *is*
different than other faiths, and I believe we need to make
sure people know what those differences are. People might
call me intolerant, but aren't they just being intolerant
of me too?

SARAH

Christians I know who claim to know all the truth make me so mad. How can they be so arrogant? What about people who were born in cultures where they grew up learning a different faith? How can we be so convinced that they aren't right too? I believe in Jesus, but I respect the rights of anyone to believe what they think is correct about God.

Rank these views from 1-4 (#1 is the view you most agree with). Why did you rank them in that order?

Placing yourself in this conversation, how can you talk respectfully with these friends about their beliefs while also expressing your own?

What are you still wondering about when it comes to this topic?

Session

6

What does the Bible say about being gay?

Big Idea

Students will dialogue about biblical and cultural approaches to the LGBT (Lesbian, Gay, Bisexual, Transgender) conversation, exploring some of the church's most complex and divisive issues of our day.

 (leader notes)

The issues surrounding sexuality and faith are especially important to young people because of the level of cultural sensitivity that has been raised in recent years. Often young people are leading the way in these conversations. Holding an open dialogue about Christian responses to the LGBT community will help your group more deeply explore the issues involved. One of the goals of this session is to help teenagers develop compassion for others and their views on this issue, as well as the experiences of real people. Allow teenagers to express or form opinions, but recognize that this session is only a beginning point, not a final conversation on human sexuality.

Also, we know there are many terms used to refer to people with same-sex attraction or who wrestle with gender identity. We will generally use terms like "LGBT" (Lesbian, Gay, Bisexual, Transgender) or "gay" in this session, but please listen for the ways your students understand and use terminology as well.

You'll Need

In (*leader notes*)

— — — — — — — — — — —

⊗ Your copy of this Leader Guide and a Student Guide for each student.

⊗ A pencil or pen for each student.

⊗ To have a good understanding of your church, denomination, or ministry organization's positions or statements about LGBT people and practices. Research this ahead of time so you can be ready to dialogue with students about this. You may want to bring copies of relevant statements. It will also be helpful to think beyond formal statements to actual postures and attitudes toward people who identify or struggle with questions of sexual identity.

Christina and Johanna grew up going to church together.

They went to camp in the summer, sat together at church on Sunday mornings, and memorized the same verses in the Bible Memory Contest in 3rd grade.

Christina and Johanna remained friends through middle school and into high school. Christina's first boyfriend was in 7th grade. She would meet him after school and they would walk downtown together. He was the first of many boyfriends for Christina.

Johanna, on the other hand, never had a boyfriend. Because they were pretty close friends, Christina would joke with her about it sometimes.

"Why don't you go for Nolan?" Christina would tease. "You'd be perfect together."

Johanna would usually change the subject.

Partway through their junior year, Christina noticed that Johanna stopped coming to church.

"Why haven't you been at church lately?" Christina asked one day.

"I just have too much to do," Johanna responded. "I'm buried in homework all the time."

Christina understood what it was like to be busy, so she didn't think much of it. But there was something else going on with Johanna that Christina didn't realize. Finally, toward the end of their junior year, Johanna decided to tell Christina her biggest secret.

One night while they were out grabbing some dinner together, Johanna told Christina that she had something important to share.

"Christina, I think I'm gay."

At first, Christina didn't know what to say. She was confused because she'd known Johanna so long and never would have guessed she was gay.

Johanna also explained that this was why she had stopped coming to church. "I know God doesn't approve of me anymore," Johanna said. "There is no way I can ever go back now."

Christina wondered, *Is it wrong to be gay and Christian? What does the Bible say about that?*

q *(questions)*

In *(leader notes)*

— — — — — — — — — — —

Acknowledge that this is a very complicated topic for most high school students. Many of them know friends, classmates, or family members who have "come out" as gay. They may have seen those same friends and family members rejected by Christians. Enter this conversation with sensitivity and compassion, regardless of your personal viewpoint. Also, recognize that someone in your group may feel just like Johanna.

You may not need to do much to get your teenagers talking about this. Caution your group about sharing stories about other people who may not want those stories shared. In particular, make sure nobody "outs" somebody else in this conversation.

Expect questions to emerge early in the discussion such as:

Are people born gay? What about genetic disposition? How could it be wrong if people are born that way?

Is there a spectrum of sexuality? Heterosexual, bisexual, homosexual, transgender—how do we navigate the changing definitions of "gay"?

These are all valid questions. Resist giving answers at this point, but instead ask for more about what they've heard about these questions. That may be insightful information for you.

> Why do you think Johanna is afraid to come back to church? Should she be afraid? Why or why not?

 (leader notes)

The book *UnChristian* shares from surveys that a major reason young people abandon church and their faith is because Christians are perceived as "anti-gay." [11] Please be aware that some of the teenagers in your group will be watching you intently to see what kind of posture you take toward the LGBT community.

> What would you say to Johanna? From your perspective, how has the LGBT (Lesbian, Gay, Bisexual, Transgender) community been treated by Christians?

 (leader notes)

Start to explore with your students the ways people who identify within the LGBT continuum have been treated in the church. What are the issues and dynamics involved in why people like Johanna might be afraid to come to church? Let your group discuss their feelings and thoughts about this.

Let them know that you will be looking at passages that discuss sexuality in the Bible in a few minutes.

(leader notes)

Next explain to your students that there is a spectrum of views on this topic among Christians. While we might wish there was "one" Christian way to understand faith and LGBT people, the diversity of views (and actual responses) is important to note. Students will find themselves in conversations like the Sticky Talk at the end of this session. If it feels helpful to use that portion of the study earlier, go for it.

> How does your church talk about sexual identity and faith?

 (leader notes)

Ask students to guess first where they think your church, denomination, or ministry organization stands on this issue. Make sure you know the answer to that, and that you have talked to your leaders about how they want this topic communicated. After students share their guesses, give them a basic overview of your church or organization's response. It's also important to note here that while we might tend to think of this as a "topic" or "issue" as a way to keep our distance from it, this conversation involves real people and their lives in deeply personal ways.

(*notes*)

THE BIBLE ON HOMOSEXUALITY

Some of the passages that address homosexuality in the Bible are Leviticus 18:22, Leviticus 20:13, 1 Corinthians 6:9-11, and 1 Timothy 1:8-10. Take a few minutes to read each passage. We'll discuss another passage in Romans 1 later.

CONTEXT!

Some scholars claim that one or more of these passages may not directly constitute a condemnation of LGBT practices, but instead are contextual to what was happening in those specific places and cultures when these parts of the Bible were written. For example, same-sex prostitution was practiced in some ancient religions. People who argue that the Bible does not prohibit homosexuality say these passages are actually addressing prohibitions against same-sex prostitution common to those religions.

Others believe the passages teach that God designed people only for relationships with the opposite sex. They also note that Jesus always taught about marriage in the context of male and female relationships, never in the context of same-sex relationships.

SLAVES, WOMEN, AND HOMOSEXUALS

A book by former pastor and professor Dr. William Webb
notes that the Bible tends to go against the cultures of its
time in these three areas in particular. Here is his argument
in a nutshell: [12]

	Slavery	Women	Homosexuality
The Culture During the Time of the Bible	The culture accepted slavery. Slaves had no rights.	Women had no rights and had many restrictions placed on them.	Homosexuality was widely accepted during this time period.
The Bible's Response	The Bible goes against culture by advocating rights for slaves.	Subverts culture by granting new freedoms. Jesus radically treated them as equals.	The Bible goes against culture – homosexuality is not mentioned positively. Jesus is silent on the issue.
What It Might Mean for Today	The Bible's teaching is used as a rationale to abolish slavery.	Many use the Bible's teaching as reasoning for full equality of women.	The Bible moves toward freedom for slavery & women's issues, but does not move toward an embrace of homosexuality.

— — —

> Do you understand Webb's argument? With what do you agree? With what do you disagree?

> Why is homosexuality emphasized so much? Some Christians are asking the question, "If Jesus never addressed homosexuality, why has this become such a big issue to some churches?" How would you respond to that question?

 (leader notes)

— — — — — — — — — — — —

Your students are growing up in a society that has pushed issues of sexual identity on them in particular ways. As you've undoubtedly noticed, the influence of media, the entertainment industry, and shifting cultural norms are all forces that have raised LGBT issues to prominence.

VIOLATING THE ORIGINAL COMMANDMENT TO HUMAN BEINGS?

Many who say the Bible is clear in its affirmation of male and female relationships alone point to the original command given to human beings to "be fruitful and multiply" (Genesis 1:28). This multiplication is not biologically possible in same-sex relationships. Others note that leaning on this passage alone also implies that single people or married people without children are sinning because they are not "multiplying."

> Can someone have feelings of same-sex attraction without being gay?

 (*leader notes*)

This question gets at the reality that sexual identity development is a process, one that ebbs and flows with teenage hormonal development and is influenced by both good and bad experiences. It also raises the question of having urges versus acting on those urges, and whether acting on same-sex urges means someone must take on a gay identity. Psychologist Mark Yarhouse shares from interviews with young Christians that some teenagers immediately assume an experience of same-sex attraction means they have a gay identity, while others do not come to that conclusion. [13] This might be important for your students to hear.

> What points on this Sticky Notes page do you find most important? Why?

> What should someone do if the Bible teaches something they disagree with?

 In *(leader notes)*

This harkens back to the authoritative role of the Bible in the life of a believer that we discussed in Session 1. Help your group process what to do when their personal convictions and the teachings of the Bible don't line up. Further, you might want to give them ideas for what students can do when they're not sure how to interpret the Bible's teachings. For example, students can talk to you or another Christian leader, find a good Bible commentary, and pray for the Holy Spirit's help.

S *(scripture)*

Romans 1:18-32 is the New Testament passage frequently cited in arguments that the Bible places homosexuality outside of God's best plan for human beings.

The wrath of God is being revealed from heaven against all the godlessness and wickedness of people, who suppress the truth by their wickedness, since what may be known about God is plain to them, because God has made it plain to them. For since the creation of the world God's invisible qualities—his eternal power and divine nature—have been clearly seen, being understood from what has been made, so that people are without excuse.

For although they knew God, they neither glorified him as God nor gave thanks to him, but their thinking became futile and their foolish hearts were darkened. Although they claimed to be wise, they became fools and exchanged the glory of the immortal God for images made to look like a mortal human being and birds and animals and reptiles.

Therefore God gave them over in the sinful desires of their hearts to sexual impurity for the degrading of their bodies with one another. They exchanged the truth about God for a lie, and worshiped and served created things rather than the Creator—who is forever praised. Amen.

Because of this, God gave them over to shameful lusts. Even their women exchanged natural sexual relations for unnatural ones. In the same way the men also abandoned natural relations with women and were inflamed with lust for one another. Men committed shameful acts with other men, and received in themselves the due penalty for their error.

Furthermore, just as they did not think it worthwhile to retain the knowledge of God, so God gave them over to a depraved mind, so that they do what ought not to be done. They have become filled with every kind of wickedness, evil, greed and depravity. They are full of envy, murder, strife, deceit and malice. They are gossips, slanderers, God-haters, insolent, arrogant and boastful; they invent ways of doing evil; they disobey their parents; they have no understanding, no fidelity, no love, no mercy. Although they know God's righteous decree that those who do such things deserve death, they not only continue to do these very things but also approve of those who practice them.

Here are two viewpoints (among many) on this passage:

Viewpoint #1: This passage makes it clear that God designed males and females for relationships with each other. Anything outside of that is unnatural according to how God created human beings. God brings judgment against people who commit sexual sin.

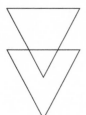

Viewpoint #2: This passage is addressing the Hellenistic culture as practiced by Romans of Paul's time that promoted worship of many gods. As part of their worship, first-century Romans practiced homosexual rituals. This passage is not speaking against LGBT people in general; it is speaking against the worship practices of that pagan culture.

> What do you think is the point of this passage? If you were going to write your viewpoint (which could be #1 or #2, or something different), what would you say?

 (leader notes)

— — — — — — — — — — — —

You may want to note in this discussion that Paul is in fact writing to a culture that worships many gods. He is illustrating how God allowed them to experience life apart from God because of their misplaced worship.

There are numerous ways we might misplace our worship; sexual expressions of all forms can be among those ways. It's easy for sex to become an idol in our culture just as much as in the Roman world.

> This passage talks about "natural" relations. Do you believe sexual orientation is something people are born with? Why or why not? How does that factor affect this conversation?

In *(leader notes)*

Some would say that if homosexuality is genetic, God can't possibly hold us accountable for an innate quality in us. Others would argue that sin is born into every human being and that, for some, one of those sins is homosexuality. If it didn't come up yet, you might also mention that it's normal for children and adolescents to experience some level of same-sex attraction, which is different from being "born gay" and also different from acting on those impulses.

> Pretend you agree with the first viewpoint above. Why do you think people with the second viewpoint believe what they do?

> Now swap your views and pretend you agree with the second viewpoint. Why do you think people who hold the first viewpoint believe what they do?

 (leader notes)

One of the goals of this session is to help teenagers develop compassion for others and their views of this issue. The two questions above might open up a conversation about how we can respectfully participate in a dialogue with others with whom we might disagree. The following section helps students practice respectful discussion, so if the swapping-viewpoint exercise doesn't work, just skip to the next section.

 (*talk*)

Pretend you are with some friends who start talking about God and sexuality. Read their viewpoints and follow the instructions below.

MONIQUE

I believe in the Bible but don't think the passages really prohibit being gay as we know it today. But there are other Christians I respect who disagree with me. I think being gay is okay because it is not hurting anyone else. Jesus never really talks about it. Don't you think that if it were really wrong, Jesus would have said something about it?

CARLOS

The culture is sliding more and more away from God, and its view on LGBT issues is just one more example. The Bible is clear in lots of places that being gay is wrong. It scares me that people are choosing to say they are Christians and yet they will not take the Bible seriously on this issue. I do not believe practicing gays can be in a right relationship with God.

TANYA

The scripture seems clear to me that God's best plan is that only men and women should be together in sexual relationships. I'm always learning about this and I'm willing to talk to people who believe differently than me. But Jesus' teaching on marriage and the first marriage in creation seem clear that this was God's intent. It breaks my heart, though, that anyone who is gay would ever feel like they are rejected.

ALAN

Jesus would never be against gay people if he were alive today. He was the most loving person ever to live. Any church that discriminates against gays and lesbians is living in ancient history. This is exactly why people don't believe in God anymore. It's because the church has become so narrow-minded and judgmental. I want to make sure the church becomes open and affirming to all people, LGBT or otherwise.

> Who do you most want to have a conversation with about this topic? What would you say or ask next?

> Who do you most agree with above?
> Write a few sentences explaining why.

> What other questions are still bugging you about this topic?

 In *(leader notes)*

Be sure to follow up individually in the coming weeks with any students who responded to this session in a way that needs more processing. For many students, this is a very personal issue and they will want to (and need to) unpack it with you further. Mark Yarhouse's *Understanding Sexual Identity: a Resource for Youth Ministry* may also be a helpful tool to help you navigate ongoing conversations.

Session

7

Does God endorse
violence?

Big Idea

Students will be exposed to scripture passages that bring into question God's view of violence, and then wrestle with these passages in light of what we find in scripture about God's love and character.

You'll Need

In *(leader notes)*

— — — — — — — — — — — —

⊗ Your copy of this Leader Guide and a Student Guide
for each participant.

⊗ A pencil or pen for each participant.

Lilly grew up in her church's children's ministry.

By the time she was in 4th grade, she had heard every children's version of a handful of Bible stories, but she didn't really start reading the Bible for herself until she was a senior in high school. Having only read the Gospels and Psalms all the way through before, she decided to start at the beginning in Genesis.

When Lilly was a kid, she had loved the Noah's Ark story. It gave her something to do with her stuffed animal collection. But now that she was reading it for herself from the "real" Bible, she realized her Sunday School teachers left out a few parts of the story that are a little less warm and fuzzy. Parts like this:

"The LORD saw that the wickedness of humankind was great in the earth, and that every inclination of the thoughts of their hearts was only evil continually. And the LORD was sorry that he had made humankind on the earth, and it grieved him to his heart. So the LORD said, "I will blot out from the earth the human beings I have created – people together with animals and creeping things and birds of the air, for I am sorry that I have made them. But Noah found favor in the sight of the LORD."
- Genesis 6:5-8 (NRSV)

A bit later, all the animals piled onto the massive boat two-by-two and sailed away into the most fun floating petting zoo the world has ever seen. But the story was different for those who weren't on the boat:

"All flesh died that moved on the earth, birds, domestic animals, wild animals, all swarming creatures that swarm on the earth, and all human beings; everything on dry land in whose nostrils was the breath of life died."
- Genesis 7:21-22 (NRSV)

━━ ━━ ━━ ━━ ━━

So while the giraffes snuggled together on the Ark, thousands of human beings (it's actually hard to say exactly how many) were being swept away in a devastating storm.

Lilly thought about that. *"All flesh died."* Dads, moms, children ... all gone.

She noticed the Bible makes it clear that this was *not* a random natural disaster like an unforeseen tsunami or a nasty tornado. This was a storm *brought on by God.*

She kept reading and noticed that the Old Testament tells more stories of God's destruction.

God destroyed the cities of Sodom and Gomorrah with "sulfur and fire" from heaven (Genesis 19), and later swallowed the entire Egyptian army in the Red Sea so that "not one of them remained" (Exodus 14), after having just killed every firstborn son in every family in Egypt. In 1 Samuel 15, the prophet Samuel commands Saul on behalf of God saying, "Go, attack the Amalekites and totally destroy all that belongs to them. Do not spare them; put to death men and women, children and infants, cattle and sheep, camels and donkeys.'" Kill them all and don't spare

anyone – *even their babies*? The Amalekites were a neighboring country; what happened to that whole "love your neighbor" thing?

Lilly began to wonder, *"What kind of violent and bloodthirsty God is this?"*

q (questions)

Have you ever heard anyone say they can't believe in a God who is violent? What was that conversation like for you?

 (leader notes)

Many students may not have a story to share. Ask them to respond to this issue from a personal perspective. **Have you ever seen the story of Noah in the light shared above? How does it make you feel? What questions does it raise?**

If we *only* had the story of Noah for context, what would you say about the character of God?

(leader notes)

Let students share some adjectives that describe God, but don't let them use anything beyond the story of Noah. Then ask, **What is the problem with just taking one story in the Bible to draw conclusions?** Nudge students to remember that we can't learn everything about the character of God from only one story. Rather, we need to take into account the entire story revealed throughout scripture.

> How does the God in the Old Testament seem different from the God in the New Testament to you?

 (leader notes)

You might hear this question from teenagers already. If the students in your group have a hard time reconciling the differences in God's actions between the Testaments, help them look at ways God was revealed over time. You might turn to examples in the Old Testament that reveal God as loving, compassionate, and willing to stick with people through their rebellion. A few passages you could read together include Isaiah 54:8-10, Jeremiah 31:1-5, and Exodus 34:5-7. Further, the Psalms are filled with great examples of God's love and patience (see Psalm 103:8-14, for example). The Old Testament primarily tells a story of God's endless pursuit of his people, and the people's tendency to rebel and to run away.

 (*notes*)

Other Viewpoints

Some have pondered stories like Noah's Ark and concluded that God is not good. Here are a couple of famous people who decided against following God, in part based on stories like Noah's.

Thomas Paine, an American revolutionary and author of *Common Sense* and *The Age of Reason*:

"Whenever we read... the cruel and tortuous executions, the unrelenting vindictiveness with which more than half the Bible is filled, it would be more consistent that we call it the word of a demon than the word of God. It is a history of wickedness that has served to corrupt and brutalize mankind; and, for my part, I sincerely detest it, as I detest everything that is cruel." [14]

Richard Dawkins, a renowned atheist:

"The God of the Old Testament is arguably the most unpleasant character in all fiction: jealous and proud of it; a petty, unjust, unforgiving control-freak; a vindictive, bloodthirsty ethnic cleanser..." [15]

> How would you respond to Thomas Paine's and Richard Dawkins' opinions?

 (leader notes)

Teenagers often become familiar with the above voices (and those like them) in high school or college. You are giving students a gift by acknowledging these voices and opening up a discussion around their points. Listen for students' own perspectives and questions, and ask how they interact with their peers when these kinds of questions arise.

Transition to the next section by saying: *Perhaps there are reasons the Bible contains stories like Noah and the destruction of the earth. Let's read a few of those reasons and see what you think.*

The Bible is Usually Raw

The Bible doesn't always soften things to make God or people who follow God look good. In many cases, the Bible simply tells the story and leaves us wondering. We witness the incredible love, grace, pain, mistakes, and yes, even blood, of real life. The Bible sometimes gives us all the gory details while leaving out answers to questions that we wish could be neatly resolved.

CONTEXT!

Many of the stories of the Old Testament take place in very brutal cultures. Few tribes and people groups had real laws. For the most part, people did whatever they wanted (or whatever their gods wanted), which included all kinds of ruthless violence. Over time, God led the Israelites to be *far more civilized* (in the ways people were treated) than surrounding nations.

For example, remember the Amalekites mentioned in the opening story (1 Samuel 15)? God didn't want the people of Israel to marry into their people and have children. Why? Like many other cultures around Israel, they had some nasty practices like sacrificing their own infants to their gods (you read that right) and killing women who were pregnant. These were not practices that aligned with the way God wanted his people to live.

In *(leader notes)*

There is a mysterious element at work in this logic. On the one hand, God is making a very clear statement against the practices of the Amalekites. On the other hand, one could argue that violence against the Amalekites just makes "two wrongs." Don't feel like you have to answer every question students pose about this; just remind them that we're looking at different sides of the issue and different ways of interpreting the stories we read.

God Responds to Sin

One thing is consistent about all the hard stories of the Old Testament: God never acts randomly. God acts against people doing wrong. As hard as it is to read some of the Old Testament stories, imagine a world where God never took action. What if God didn't care that the Amalekites were sacrificing their children? Is that the kind of God you'd want to follow?

 (leader notes)

Students may ask the question, "If that's true, then why doesn't God always respond?" This question opens up the larger problem of evil. Encourage your group for asking this difficult question. While we can't possibly account for why God sometimes responds to wrong and sometimes does not, we can encourage students to consider several important aspects of God's acts and character:

1. God gave us the ability to make choices. As part of God's love for us, we can choose whether or not to love God and obey him. This choice means rebellion is an option for anyone.

2. God does not sit back and watch us suffer. Jesus entered our suffering in the flesh, enduring intense human pain and loss when he died on the cross.

3. God will ultimately establish justice and make all things right. Scripture promises that in the end, all tears will be wiped away and all creation will be made new (Revelation 21). This also means evil will be judged (Revelation 20:11-15).

God's Unlikely Love and Patience Seem to be EVERYWHERE in the Old and New Testaments

The Bible is filled with stories of God's patience and love. Over and over again, God loves people who don't deserve it. Jonah is a great example. It's tempting to focus on the sleepover in the fish belly, but don't miss the rest of the narrative. God asked Jonah to go to Nineveh (a city considered very anti-God at the time) and invite them to follow God. Jonah didn't like that idea and tried to go as far away as possible – to a place called Tarshish. When God finally led him to Nineveh, Jonah was still upset. He *hated* the people there. Even after they responded to the message and turned away from evil, Jonah was ticked. Don't believe us? Check this out:

> *Jonah was furious. He lost his temper. He yelled at GOD, "GOD! I knew it—when I was back home, I knew this was going to happen! That's why I ran off to Tarshish! I knew you were sheer grace and mercy, not easily angered, rich in love, and ready at the drop of a hat to turn your plans of punishment into a program of forgiveness!* — Jonah 4:1-2 (The Message)

Read those two verses again carefully. The words *"I knew it..."* are really important. Despite the fact some want to portray God as cruel, comments like Jonah's make it clear God had a reputation for loving people who didn't deserve it. This becomes even more evident when Jesus comes on the scene.

> Which of these points do you think is most important on this topic? Why?

 (leader notes)

You could discuss one or more of the previously mentioned Old Testament passages about God's patient love (Isaiah 54:8-10, Jeremiah 31:1-5, Exodus 34:5-7, and Psalm 103:8-14) if you did not already read them.

According to Scripture, Jesus Gives Us the Clearest Picture of God

In Colossians 1, Jesus is described as the "visible image of the invisible God." Jesus was God himself, who came to earth as a human being or, as some like to say, he was "God in the bod." That means whenever he opens his mouth or reacts to a situation, *you get to see God in action.* If you want to know God, know Jesus. So the question then becomes, "Is Jesus violent?"

> Which of these points do you think is most important? Why?

 (leader notes)

Emphasize our ability to observe Jesus in the stories of the New Testament and see more about the heart of God. The next section gives students that opportunity.

S (scripture)

Many people in the first century expected, based in part on the stories from the Old Testament, that Jesus would lead a military campaign to defeat the Romans (who had taken over Israel). They expected a rebellion headed by an amazing fighter. What they got instead was a God who chose to be born in humble circumstances in the middle of nowhere. Jesus grew up in a common family of his time, helping to build furniture to survive. While many religious people of the day expected a great warrior, God came to earth in a way that no one expected – as a poor, compassionate carpenter-turned-teacher named Jesus. He lived and loved people in a way that, according to the gospel of Mark, announced the Kingdom of God (Mark 1:15). This kingdom would be different than the kingdoms of earth. When the time came that some people in power wanted Jesus dead, the creator of the universe had a choice: would he use his unlimited power to destroy his enemies? Or would he lay his power aside and allow himself to be sacrificed?

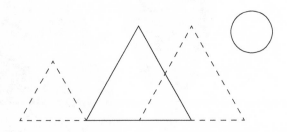

While he was still speaking, Judas, one of the Twelve, arrived. With him was a large crowd armed with swords and clubs, sent from the chief priests and the elders of the people. Now the betrayer had arranged a signal with them: "The one I kiss is the man; arrest him." Going at once to Jesus, Judas said, "Greetings, Rabbi!" and kissed him.

Jesus replied, "Do what you came for, friend."

Then the men stepped forward, seized Jesus and arrested him. With that, one of Jesus' companions reached for his sword, drew it out and struck the servant of the high priest, cutting off his ear.

"Put your sword back in its place," Jesus said to him, "for all who draw the sword will die by the sword. Do you think I cannot call on my Father, and he will at once put at my disposal more than twelve legions of angels? But how then would the Scriptures be fulfilled that say it must happen in this way?"

> In that hour Jesus said to the crowd, "Am I leading
> a rebellion, that you have come out with swords
> and clubs to capture me? Every day I sat in the
> temple courts teaching, and you did not arrest me.
> But this has all taken place that the writings of the
> prophets might be fulfilled." Then all the disciples
> deserted him and fled.
>
> — Matthew 26:47-56

What is Jesus' reaction toward violence in this passage?

Assume for a moment that Jesus was all-powerful and could have wiped out the Romans with his angel army (by the way – a legion is 6,000 soldiers. Do the math: that's a lot of angels). Why didn't he do it?

In *(leader notes)*

— — — — — — — — — — — —

Personalize the topic by asking, "How hard would it be for you not to use violence if you had been in Jesus' situation?"

What does this passage tell you about God's character?

In *(leader notes)*

— — — — — — — — — — — — —

Again, if Jesus is God in the flesh, we can see the character of God come out in everything he does. Jesus is embodying what many writers of the Old Testament "knew." God is incredibly loving and patient. We are now seeing the full expression of that in Jesus.

> What other stories from the New Testament give us an idea about how Jesus viewed violence? (If you need a hint, check out Matthew 19, John 2, or John 11.)

In *(leader notes)*

— — — — — — — — — — — — —

Jesus becomes angry in a few passages of the Bible:

1. When children are prevented from seeing him (Matthew 19)

2. The cleansing of the temple (John 2)

3. The death of Lazarus (John 11)

It might be helpful to note that anger is not always bad. Why someone becomes angry, and what they do in response, reveal a lot. Note that Jesus becomes angry when other people are harmed. Yet Jesus never strikes vengefully when he himself is wronged.

In terms of Jesus acting out in violence, the closest thing we find is John 2:15. During the "cleansing of the temple," Jesus makes a whip and knocks over tables to help stop the money changing in the temple. This shows the depth of his anger at injustice and misplaced worship.

Pretend you are with some friends who start talking about God. Read their viewpoints and follow the instructions below.

CHRISTINA

It's hard to defend how angry God gets. You can see it in the Old Testament. Those stories are really brutal – it makes me sometimes wonder how we can follow a God like that. I heard someone say once that the evil things Christians have done in human history are just people imitating what they saw God do in the Old Testament. We say we hate Adolf Hitler who killed all those people. Hasn't God done the same thing? How do we justify that?

The next session focuses on evil acts led by Christians, so resist going too deep in that conversation here. This will help get them thinking about it!

THOMAS

God is real, but I think he is kind of "distant." It's not that God is so cruel and mean. He's just not around. Those stories in the Old Testament were just the people's perceptions of what God wanted. He didn't really want them to kill the Amalekites, but the people used God as an excuse to do it. The truth is that God is not involved in the everyday lives of human beings. He made the world and then stepped back and let us make our own choices. When is the last time you really saw God do something good or bad?

JANET

God is in my life doing good every day. Every breath, every
smile, every time I see something beautiful, I don't take
it for granted that God made those things and made me to
enjoy them. Jesus changed the world precisely by *not* being
violent. He showed God's true character. I will admit that
I don't understand all the Old Testament stories and they
seem confusing, but I know that was a different culture
than the world we live in today. I also know that Jesus has
earned my trust – I'm guessing there may be more to those
stories than I'll ever know.

CALVIN

I don't think people should question how God acts in the
Bible so much. God's decisions are too hard for our little
minds to understand. Doubting God about something like this
will lead to doubt in other ways too. Why can't we just
admit that we can't figure out everything God does and be
okay with that?

Who do you relate to the *least*? Why?

What other questions do you have right now
about this topic?

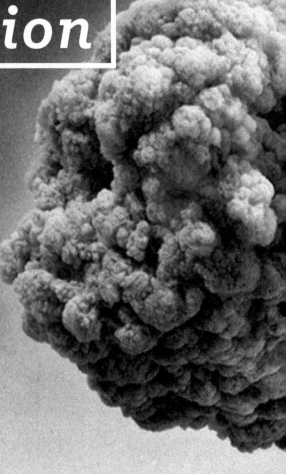

Session

8

*How can
I follow a
God who
would let
Christians
do such
bad things?*

Big Idea

Students will explore whether the acts of some people who are (or claim to be) Christians invalidate the ministry and claims of Jesus. This session also aims to give students exposure to some of the incredible contributions followers of Jesus have made to world history.

You'll Need

In *(leader notes)*

- ⊗ Your copy of this Leader Guide and a Student Guide for each participant.

- ⊗ A pencil or pen for each participant.

It was game four of the World Series and the Chicago Cubs had a chance to sweep the Yankees.

As the game went on, the most important news stories of the evening scrolled by on the bottom of the screen. One news item read:

"Famous pastor admits to cheating on wife and stealing money from church – will face charges..."

Charley's friend Josh almost choked on a nacho chip.

"I'm so sick of these hypocritical Christians!" Josh yelled. "They are supposed to be these perfect people, but they're the ones who are doing the worst things."

Charley had gone to church for just over a year now, and thought the youth group was pretty fun. He was trying to learn about God, but it was easy to get confused by stuff like this. His friend Kirsten was the one who invited him to church. She was watching the game with them and chimed in.

"You need to calm down, Josh," she said. "Christians aren't perfect, they are just forgiven."

"I'm sick of reading that stupid bumper sticker, and I think it's an excuse to behave badly," Josh said, growing visibly angry. "Think of all the terrible things that Christians have done over the course of history: The Crusades, The Spanish Inquisition, the killing of Native Americans, and slavery. Even Hitler said he was a Christian and that was one reason to get rid of the Jews. How can you possibly say you are one of *them*?"

The fun World Series viewing party had turned awkward.

"You have all your facts mixed up, Josh," she said. "Are you claiming to be perfect? Do you never make mistakes?"

"Of course I make mistakes," Josh replied. "But I don't need to use Jesus as an excuse for the dumb things I do."

Charley turned the television's volume all the way up as a humorous attempt at getting them to quit arguing. But he kept thinking about the conversation later. He didn't want to be associated with people who did horrible things.

Charley wondered, *"Why would God let Christians do such terrible things?"*

q *(questions)*

> When have you thought about this question before?

In *(leader notes)*

— — — — — — — — — — — —

Your group will likely bring up more recent examples of those who claim to be Christians who have done wrong. Use this question to gauge the engagement level of your group on this topic.

> What do you notice about the argument between Josh and Kirsten? Are they handling this conversation well? Why or why not?

(leader notes)

— — — — — — — — — — — —

The problem with Kirsten's response is that it can sound to others like, *"Christians can get away with anything because God forgives."* A key point to coax from your group during this question (or in one of the next questions): It's important to realize that people have often used Christianity to their advantage to get what they want.

> Does Josh have his facts straight? What would you say to Josh?

 (leader notes)

— — — — — — — — — — — —

While some individuals or groups of Christianity have indeed done really terrible things (sometimes in Jesus' name), it's important to point out that we need to be careful with one-sided arguments. While some Christians used the Bible to continue the practice of slavery or harm other people, others used the Bible as their ultimate justification for fighting those same things.

> Talk to someone this week and ask them about this topic – preferably someone who may not consider themselves a Christian. How do they feel about this?

(notes)

More Sides to the Story

While we can focus on some of the awful things done by Christians in history, those who have followed Jesus' lead have also been responsible for some incredible gifts to humanity. Consider these examples of issues where Christians have led the way in helping others: [16]

Children: *In ancient times, children were often not named for over a week in case the parents decided to dispose of the baby. The early Christian church helped change this practice because of Jesus' love for children (Matthew 19:14).*

Medical care: *Followers of Jesus founded many of the great health care systems in the world. Our hospitals, many of which are named after the disciples or characters in the scriptures (St. Luke's and Good Samaritan are common examples), are a reminder of that tradition. They were inspired by Jesus' words, "Whatever you do for the least of these, you do for me ..." (Matthew 25:40).*

Higher Learning: *Many of the world's greatest universities started with Jesus' teaching in mind. Schools like Oxford, Cambridge, Harvard, Stanford and Yale have their roots in Christianity. In fact, ninety-two percent of the first 138 universities founded in America were started by followers of Jesus. Jesus said, "Love the Lord Your God with all your ... mind." (Luke 10:27).*

Slavery and Civil Rights: *Some of the greatest human rights leaders of our time, including William Wilberforce in England and Martin Luther King Jr. in the United States, passionately pursued racial equality because of Jesus' teaching. The apostle Paul wrote, "There is no longer Jew or Greek, there is no longer slave or free, there is no longer male and female; for all of you are one in Christ Jesus." (Galatians 3:28). Some people have called this the first written statement of human equality in all of human history.*

Ethics: *"Humility" was not thought of as something positive in the time and culture Jesus lived in. Yet later Paul would write, "He humbled himself and became obedient to the point of death – even death on a cross." (Philippians 2:8). Jesus and the writers of the New Testament radically went against the ethic of taking revenge on others. Jesus said, "Love your enemies and pray for those who persecute you ..." (Matthew 5:44). The author of 1 Peter wrote, "Do not repay evil for evil or abuse for abuse; but, on the contrary, repay with a blessing." (1 Peter 3:9). The humility of Jesus has been the hallmark and inspiration of Christians like Mother Teresa (who served the poorest of the poor in Calcutta, India, for many years) and others who have sought to follow Jesus' example of serving rather than being served (see John 13 for a powerful story about Jesus washing his friends' feet).*

 (leader notes)

Your group might be surprised by some of this. Ask for their impressions about these examples. How does this help balance out the story of Christians' behavior and its reflection on God?

Join the Argument

Christians often spend time defending the terrible things some people have done in the name of Christianity. Instead of defending the actions of Christians who have done evil, it is often best to agree that those actions don't represent Jesus.

 (leader notes)

Help release students from the pressure to defend the acts of some Christians that are completely indefensible.

The Ironic Origin of the Word "Hypocrite"

Pastor and writer John Ortberg notes that the origin of the word "hypocrite" actually comes from Jesus himself. [17] Jesus uses that word 17 times in the New Testament. He constantly criticized religious leaders who said one thing, but did another. So sometimes it's totally appropriate to call out hypocrisy for what it is.

> Mahatma Gandhi once said of Christianity: "I like your Christ, I do not like your Christians. Your Christians are so unlike your Christ." Is it possible to change the perception of Christians that many unchurched people have? How?

 (leader notes)

Help your group to see the importance of a life lived in honor of Jesus Christ that is a witness to the world of who Jesus Christ really is.

(*scripture*)

Jesus had a lot to say about how we live our lives. A disciple is someone who follows "the way" of someone else. Jesus invited us to be his disciples. He also warned that many people would claim to be his followers but were not genuine disciples. Read these words from Jesus' famous "Sermon on the Mount":

Watch out for false prophets. They come to you in sheep's clothing, but inwardly they are ferocious wolves. By their fruit you will recognize them. Do people pick grapes from thornbushes, or figs from thistles? Likewise, every good tree bears good fruit, but a bad tree bears bad fruit. A good tree cannot bear bad fruit, and a bad tree cannot bear good fruit. Every tree that does not bear good fruit is cut down and thrown into the fire. Thus, by their fruit you will recognize them.

— Matthew 7:15-20

Jesus says we will be able to tell false leaders "by their fruit." What do you think that means?

(*leader notes*)

One way to answer this could be to look at the fruit of the Spirit in Galatians 5:22. Does the person's work and teaching seem to lead to these things?

> Have you ever experienced someone using Jesus or Christianity as a justification to do wrong?

 (*leader notes*)

Move on if you've already covered this.

> Do you think people in the church can be easily led down the wrong path by false teaching? Why? How could that be prevented?

 (*leader notes*)

This is an opportunity to help students see how critical the Bible is in the formation of a follower of Jesus. To identify what is false, it helps to know intimately what is genuine. We do that by knowing Jesus Christ as presented in the scriptures.

BONUS Scripture...

The book of James in the New Testament stresses the importance of not just knowing about the way of Jesus. James encourages us to actually *live* like we know Jesus.

> *Do not merely listen to the word, and so deceive yourselves. Do what it says. Anyone who listens to the word but does not do what it says is like someone who looks at his face in a mirror and, after looking at himself, goes away and immediately forgets what he looks like. But whoever looks intently into the perfect law that gives freedom, and continues in it—not forgetting what they have heard, but doing it—they will be blessed in what they do.* — James 1:22-25

What do you think is the main point of this passage?

> Describe someone who lives in a way that makes it obvious they love Jesus. How do you think that person came to be that way?

 (leader notes)

This might be a good opportunity to describe spiritual practices that help us grow in our faith. At their best, disciplines like prayer, Bible study, and worship are avenues through which the Holy Spirit forms the character of Jesus Christ in us. Share from your own experience and suggest a few ideas that might be good starting points for your students.

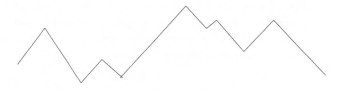

(talk)

Pretend some friends post Facebook status updates like the ones below. Write your own short response in the comment boxes under each post.

Vicki

My professor today talked about the ways in which slave owners in the South cited passages in the Bible to justify keeping slaves. This was just one more example to me of how Christians have done terrible things. I sometimes wonder if the world would be a better place if there were no religions. Think about how many religious wars there have been!

Like · Comment · Share · 34 minutes ago

Jeremy

i'm embarrassed by the stupid things some people have done who claimed to be christians. but, i guess I've done some pretty dumb things too... i know we all need forgiveness. i just wish people could separate the teachings of Jesus from the bad things christians have done. i'm sad people are missing out on Jesus because they get stuck on christians' failures.

Like · Comment · Share · 2 minutes ago

Henry

I'm tired of people saying that Christians are bad. Are you kidding me? Without Christians, the entire world as we know it would be a mess. Civilizations that have looked to Jesus as their source of ethics are far more advanced in civil rights than civilizations that haven't. I am happy to defend the record of Christians in history.

Like · Comment · Share · 41 minutes ago

Joan

I see that Christians have done terrible things. I also see they have done good things. So... I don't understand why Christianity is necessary to live a good life. Some of the most ethical, wonderful people I know are not Christians. Shouldn't we just love each other regardless if someone is a Christian? why follow any religion? I can be ethical all by myself

Like · Comment · Share · 17 minutes ago

What's still bugging you about this topic?

10 Tips for reading your Bible

Hopefully this study has left you hungry to learn and grow more in your faith in God. One way to do that is by reading your Bible. Like anything worth doing, it takes some practice and time to know how to read it well. Here are a few tips on how you can get started or make your attempts at reading the Bible more meaningful.

1

Pray for the Spirit to Help You

You will not be able to understand the Bible well without God's help. Pray for the Holy Spirit to guide you when you read. Jesus told his followers, "When the Spirit of truth comes, he will guide you into all truth ..." (John 16:13). Take Jesus up on this promise and invite God to lead you. *Ask God to give you a heart that is open to being changed.*

Formation vs. Information

2

To read the Bible and grow from it, you need to learn a different way to read. In school, you usually read for "information." Reading for school often means you need to read as much as you can as fast as you can. Why? Two words: FINAL EXAM.

But reading the Bible is more about "formation" than information. God is using the Bible to shape or *form* you into a new person. That doesn't happen by reading as fast as you can and trying to memorize facts. With the Bible, it's often just the opposite. Read the Bible slowly. Pray as you go. Stop and ask questions. There is no pressure to "get through it." *If you are just trying to get through the Bible, the Bible won't get through to you.*

No Shame ┌─┐ 3

High school is often the first time people start to feel shame that they don't know much about the Bible. Don't fall into the trap of thinking everyone knows how to read the Bible except you. Many adults, probably even those who go to your church, don't know how to read it well.

Sometimes high schoolers feel like they are so "far behind" when it comes to Bible knowledge that they don't even try. Don't be afraid to be honest about what you do and don't understand about the Bible, and ask for help from a trusted leader (see #7 below).

Get a Readable Bible

Did you know there are all kinds of Bible translations out there? Make sure your Bible has words that are easily understandable. The King James Version may not be your best choice, because it was translated in a language popular centuries ago. Some translations that are easier for students to read include the *New International Version* (NIV), *Common English Bible* (CEB), *New Revised Standard Version* (NRSV), or the *New Living Translation* (NLT). You might also want to look for a Bible that has extra notes for context, sometimes called a "Study Bible." Some of these are written especially for teenagers. Most of the excerpts in this study have been from the NIV translation, with a few from *The Message* (which utilizes modern phrases and expressions to communicate in today's language as much as possible).

Don't Start at Start

Jim remembers getting his first Bible, opening it, and starting to read it just like every book he'd ever read; from the beginning to the end. He made it to Exodus before he quit. If you've never read the Bible before, *you may not want to start in Genesis*. Read one of the gospels first (Matthew, Mark, Luke, or John). Those books tell Jesus' story and are a great place to get started. Then go back and get a sense for the bigger story from Creation to New Creation (Genesis to Revelation).

Read the Notes Before the Book

A good Bible will often include notes that introduce each book. It is good to read those notes before you dive in. Bibles with a good introduction will help you understand the context of what you are reading. Context is important because it tells you who is writing to whom and why they are writing.

Bible Reading is a "Team Sport"

When you begin reading the Bible, you will be confused at times. *That is okay.* Read with someone else who knows the Bible more than you do. Find a pastor at your church, another Christian group leader, a parent or a friend who knows the Bible and can help you. Don't struggle through the Bible on your own!

Use Your Imagination **8**

The Bible tells some of the greatest stories you'll ever read. It also does not always elaborate on important elements of those stories. Stop when you read stories in the Bible and ask questions like, "What was the person thinking and feeling? What would it have been like to be there?" Use your imagination when you read the Bible.

Stick With it

Many people start the Bible, get confused, and quit. Don't let that be you. If you are confused, remember that you're not alone. Reading the Bible is much like learning to play an instrument or a new sport. The more you practice reading it, the more natural it will become. Don't give up.

9

It's About God

The Bible is not a "nice road map" with good tips on how to live. The Bible is a collection of stories, poems, songs, and letters that work together to tell one big story about God and about us. There *are* great thoughts about living your life, but the goal of the Bible is to reveal God, and to draw you into a relationship with God. Get to know God as you read it.

Insider Tips

⊗ There are two major sections of the Bible: The Old and New Testaments. The Old Testament tells the story of creation, of the journeys of God's people, and of their anticipation of the coming of Jesus. It also includes books like the Psalms, which capture poetry and songs that span the breadth of human emotion and response to God. The New Testament tells the story of Jesus on earth and what his life, death and resurrection mean. It goes on to share about the earliest churches and some of their letters to one another about living out the way of Jesus together. It closes with visions of Jesus returning to make all things new, and a promise that he will bring those visions to reality some day.

⊗ The Bible is broken into chapters and verses. John 3:16 refers to a verse in the gospel of John, chapter 3, verse 16. The little numbers you find in the midst of the paragraphs and sentences are verse numbers and make things easier to find. Many Bibles include footnotes that refer you to other passages where you find a similar verse, idea, or an exact quote that is repeated by another author. Sometimes that can help you piece together the different parts of the story.

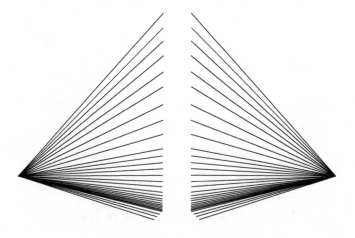

⊗ The Gospels are the four books that start the New Testament (Matthew, Mark, Luke, and John) and tell the story of Jesus. The word *gospel* means "good news."

Letter for Parents

Dear Parents,

I'm writing to let you know about an important study we are beginning with high school students.

We will be using a resource titled Can I Ask That?, a Sticky Faith curriculum from the Fuller Youth Institute (fulleryouthinstitute.org), that is designed to lead teenagers in critical conversations about their faith. This study will invite students to look at topics like evolution, the reliability of the Bible, and homosexuality. It raises hard questions that don't have easy answers, and helps students think about them from a biblical perspective.

We have a conviction that high schoolers should wrestle with challenging topics now, with adults who know them and care about their faith, rather than on their own later. Some research suggests that about 50 percent of youth group participants will leave their faith when they graduate from high school (see stickyfaith.org for more research and resources addressing this concern). We don't want young people to leave faith in Christ because we haven't had real conversations with them about topics that matter.

The studies are written to intentionally encourage students to consider many sides of these issues and help them begin to form their own opinions based on dialogue around scripture, different Christian and non-Christian perspectives, and the tradition of our church. If you are interested in a copy of the curriculum, please let us know. We always welcome your questions and input.

Also, would you please pray for this study? We believe it has the potential to lead to great breakthroughs for a lot of our young people. We'd be grateful if you asked God to help make that happen.

Thanks for allowing us to partner with you to grow and strengthen the spiritual lives of your kids.

Blessings,

Footnotes

1. Larry Alex Taunton, "Listening to Young Atheists: Lessons for a Stronger Christianity," *The Atlantic*, June 6, 2013.

2. This list and the telephone viewpoint are compiled from various sources and represent the thoughts of New Testament scholars such as Bart Ehrman. See ehrmanblog.org or Bart Ehrman, *Misquoting Jesus: The Story Behind Who Changed the Bible and Why* (San Francisco: HarperOne, 2007).

3. To explore more scholarly work on biblical variances, see Bruce Metzger, *The Early Versions of the New Testament: Their Origin, Transmission, and Limitations* (New York: Oxford University Press, 1977). Also F.F. Bruce, *The Canon of Scripture* (Downers Grove, IL: InterVarsity Press, 1988).

4. For more on the development of the canon see Bruce Metzger, *The Canon of the New Testament: Its Origin, Development, and Significance* (New York: Oxford University Press, 1997).

5. John W. Montgomery, *History and Christianity* (Downers Grove, IL: InterVarsity Press, 1971), 29.

6. From a lecture in 2007 at Stanford University titled "*Misquoting Jesus, Stanford Lecture, How the Bible Got Tainted.*"

7. F. F. Bruce, *The New Testament Documents: Are They Reliable?* 15.

8. C.S. Lewis, *Mere Christianity* (New York: Macmillan Publishing, 1942), 121.

9. John MacArthur, *The Battle for the Beginning* (Nashville: Thomas Nelson, 2001), 29.

10. Gary Burge has a good explanation of this in *The NIV Application Commentary: John.* p. 407

11. See David Kinnaman and Gabe Lyons, *unchristian: What a new generation really thinks about Christianity ... and Why it matters* (Grand Rapids: Baker Books, 2007).

12. William J. Webb, *Slaves, Women, & Homosexuals: Exploring the Hermeneutics of Cultural Analysis* (Downers Grove, IL: InterVarsity Press, 2001).

13. See Mark Yarhouse, *Understanding Sexual Identity: A Resource for Youth Ministry* (Grand Rapids: Zondervan, 2013), in particular chapter 3.

14. Paine, Thomas. *The Age of Reason.* Ed. Kerry Walters (Peterborough: Broadview Press, 2011), Part 1, Section IV.

15. Dawkins, Richard. *The God Delusion* (New York: Houghton Mifflin, 2006), 31.

16. These summaries are adapted from John Ortberg's *Who is This Man?: The Unpredictable Impact of the Inescapable Jesus.* (Grand Rapids: Zondervan, 2012).

17. John Ortberg, *Who is this Man?* (Grand Rapids: Zondervan, 2012), 119.

Photos